Praise for *Don't Miss the Moment*

"If you have ever found yourself thinking God has forgotten about you, Don't Miss the Moment is for you. It will help you see God's faithfulness in your everyday life even when things aren't going how you had hoped or planned."

—CHRISTINE CAINE, BESTSELLING AUTHOR,
FOUNDER A21 AND PROPEL WOMEN

"The incredible Pastor Sheryl Brady encourages us to be fearless and patient when things do not go our way. This book is for anyone looking to surrender themselves to faith, especially in the face of failure and doubt!"

—DEVON FRANKLIN, HOLLYWOOD PRODUCER AND
NEW YORK TIMES BESTSELLING AUTHOR

"Pastor Sheryl Brady passionately teaches us how to recognize, appreciate, and embrace our life experiences ('moments') for what they are designed to ultimately produce. If only I knew then what I know now, I would have recognized sooner that the death of my six-month-old, premature daughter was a moment to be seized. Through laughter and tears, I've now come to understand the purpose behind my moments. Thanks to Sheryl, I won't miss another one!"

—CYNT MARSHALL, CEO, DALLAS MAVERICKS

"Sheryl draws from her life experiences to remind us that nothing we go though in life is wasted. Even though things may appear to be out of our control and setbacks seem to be inevitable, EVERY moment is holy and can be redeemed for God's glory"

—SAMUEL RODRIGUEZ, NEW SEASON LEAD PASTOR,
NHCLC PRESIDENT, AUTHOR OF *YOU ARE NEXT!*,
EXECUTIVE PRODUCER OF THE MOVIE *BREAKTHROUGH*

"Pastor Sheryl Brady invokes us to reminisce over our lives when time stood still allowing our hearts to ingest periods of success or failure—excellence or defeat, fame or loss. Inhale and Don't Miss the Moment."

—SERITA JAKES, AUTHOR OF *THE PRINCESS WITHIN*

"Pastor Sheryl Brady is a lover of people, especially those who have been broken and discarded. This book is about love and grace in motion, and who better to talk about that than someone whose life shouts love and grace."

—PAUL SCANLON, AUTHOR AND MOTIVATIONAL SPEAKER

"Many of us live life on fast forward. We have our eyes so focused on the future, that we miss the beauty of the wisdom unfolding itself before us every day. This powerful book is a must-read for anyone who wants to reach the end of life confident that their life was well lived."

—NONA JONES, GLOBAL FAITH-BASED PARTNERSHIPS, FACEBOOK; AUTHOR OF *SUCCESS FROM THE INSIDE OUT*

"All of life is about managing the moment you are in. In this book Pastor Sheryl Brady makes us the beneficiaries of her rich life experiences. Her journey will certainly help us not to underestimate the importance of the moments that God has given us."

—BISHOP MICHAEL PITTS, FOUNDER OF CORNERSTONE CHURCH TOLEDO

"Sheryl Brady reminds us that perspective is everything and that God wants to speak to us through the most seemingly insignificant ways."

—REGGIE JOINER, FOUNDER AND CEO, ORANGE

"I love Sheryl Brady. Her joy and love for God is infectious! *Don't Miss the Moment* encourages us to see God bigger and more than we have ever seen Him before. His greatness shows up in moments that will change your destiny!"

—CeCe Winans, Grammy Award-winning artist

"Sheryl is a woman worth following. This book becomes a guide for us all as we navigate the moments, big and small, in our own lives and how they are part of the bigger picture God sees."

—Carey Nieuwhof, bestselling author of *Didn't See It Coming*; founding pastor, Connexus Church

"Pastor Sheryl reminds us that some of the most seemingly insignificant 'God moments' are the ones that totally catch us by surprise. Learn to acknowledge these small moments and appreciate that God truly delights in every detail of your life!"

—Nicole Crank, senior pastor, FaithChurch.com— St. Louis, Royal Palm, and West Palm Beach

"This book masterfully reminds us of the power of moments, the importance of recognizing them, and the necessity of stewarding them well. More than a book, this is a road map and a blueprint that will help you walk into your destiny one moment at a time."

—Dharius Daniels, pastor, Change Church; author, *Relational Intelligence*

"I recommend this book for anyone who has ever wondered about God's plan for their life. Despite challenges and obstacles, you will be encouraged to capture the moment and to press on!"

—Pastor John K. Jenkins Sr., First Baptist Church of Glenarden, Maryland

Don't Miss
the Moment

How God Uses the Insignificant to Create the Extraordinary

Sheryl Brady

NELSON
BOOKS

An Imprint of Thomas Nelson

Published in Nashville, Tennessee, by Nelson Books, an imprint of Thomas Nelson. Nelson Books and Thomas Nelson are registered trademarks of HarperCollins Christian Publishing, Inc.

Thomas Nelson titles may be purchased in bulk for educational, business, fund-raising, or sales promotional use. For information, please e-mail SpecialMarkets@ThomasNelson.com.

Unless otherwise noted, Scripture quotations are taken from the Holy Bible, New International Version®, NIV®. Copyright © 1973, 1978, 1984, 2011 by Biblica, Inc.® Used by permission of Zondervan. All rights reserved worldwide. www.Zondervan.com. The "NIV" and "New International Version" are trademarks registered in the United States Patent and Trademark Office by Biblica, Inc.® Scripture quotations marked AMP are from the Amplified® Bible. Copyright © 1954, 1958, 1962, 1964, 1965, 1987 by The Lockman Foundation. Used by permission. (www.Lockman.org) Scripture quotations marked KJV are from the King James Version. Public domain. Scripture quotations marked THE MESSAGE are from *The Message*. Copyright © by Eugene H. Peterson 1993, 1994, 1995, 1996, 2000, 2001, 2002. Used by permission of NavPress. All rights reserved. Represented by Tyndale House Publishers, Inc. Scripture quotations marked NKJV are from the New King James Version®. © 1982 by Thomas Nelson. Used by permission. All rights reserved. Scripture quotations marked NLT are from the Holy Bible, New Living Translation. © 1996, 2004, 2007, 2013, 2015 by Tyndale House Foundation. Used by permission of Tyndale House Publishers, Inc., Carol Stream, Illinois 60188. All rights reserved. Scripture quotations marked TPT are from The Passion Translation®. Copyright © 2017 by BroadStreet Publishing® Group, LLC. Used by permission. All rights reserved. thePassionTranslation.com. Scripture quotations marked THE VOICE are from The Voice™. © 2012 by Ecclesia Bible Society. Used by permission. All rights reserved. Note: Italics in quotations from The Voice are used to "indicate words not directly tied to the dynamic translation of the original language" but that "bring out the nuance of the original, assist in completing ideas, and . . . provide readers with information that would have been obvious to the original audience" (The Voice, preface).

Any Internet addresses, phone numbers, or company or product information printed in this book are offered as a resource and are not intended in any way to be or to imply an endorsement by Thomas Nelson, nor does Thomas Nelson vouch for the existence, content, or services of these sites, phone numbers, companies, or products beyond the life of this book.

ISBN 978–1–4002–1049–7 (eBook)
ISBN 978–1–4002–0184–6 (HC)
ISBN 978–1–4002–0885–2 (IE)

Library of Congress Cataloging-in-Publication Data

Names: Brady, Sheryl, 1960- author.
Title: Don't miss the moment : how God uses the insignificant to create the
    extraordinary / Sheryl Brady.
Description: Nashville : Thomas Nelson, 2020. | Includes bibliographical
    references. | Summary: "Pastor and popular Bible teacher Sheryl Brady
    helps Christians prepare for, recognize, and cultivate the powerful yet
    easily overlooked moments when God shows up in their lives"-- Provided
    by publisher.
Identifiers: LCCN 2019034402 (print) | LCCN 2019034403 (ebook) | ISBN
    9781400201846 (hardcover) | ISBN 9781400201860 (ebook)
Subjects: LCSH: Spirituality--Christianity. | Relevance--Miscellanea.
Classification: LCC BV4501.3 .B74214 2020 (print) | LCC BV4501.3 (ebook)
    | DDC 248.4--dc23
LC record available at https://lccn.loc.gov/2019034402
LC ebook record available at https://lccn.loc.gov/2019034403

Printed in the United States of America

20 21 22 23 24 LSC 10 9 8 7 6 5 4 3 2 1

I dedicate this book to

My sister, Elaine:
  One of the richest blessings that Mom and Dad gave me was you. The tenderness and pure kindness that radiates from your heart is everything I have always imagined the heart of Jesus would look like. The strength of your hugs are like none other. You have modeled Jesus all day, every day of my life. I want to be just like you when I grow up.

My daughters, Lana, Tina, and Nina:
  I was the first person to get to touch you. I snuggled up to you, held you close, and kept you warm. I rubbed your cheeks against mine, and I whispered things in your ears that will forever be our secret. I gave you my finger and you instantly wrapped your little hand around it. I knew then that we were connected for all eternity.
  As I looked into the most beautiful faces God had ever created my prayer was that he would always let me be there for you. That he would allow me to steady you while life taught you the lessons you would need to learn. He has answered my prayer. I have watched you grow into GREAT women of God. I've watched you ROCK your marriages, your families, your ministries, your careers, and become role models for women everywhere.

You have become more than my children . . . you are heaven's gifts to me. You are my prayer partners, my ministry partners, my pride and joy, my friends, and, most of all, you're my "threefold cord" that never has been, nor ever will be easily broken. You have by far been the richest soil God has allowed me to sow into. You are proof that his law of reciprocity even works in families. I am reaping! And as with any seed, I am reaping much more than I have ever sown. And now, it is YOU who wraps me up. You are the ones who hold me close. You are keeping me warm and it is the words you have whispered in my ear that continue to steady me in the shakiest moments of my life.

I have no idea what I've done to DESERVE YOU, but I will seize every moment of every day thanking God FOR YOU!

My granddaughters, McKenzie, Sydney, and Mariah:

I am captivated as I watch the mighty hand of God unearth and unveil the unique treasure trove of ministry that was yours before you drew your first breath. You are called and chosen. There is a generational anointing that is behind you, pushing you to seize your moment. You will go places I've never gone, do things I've never done, and see things I've never seen. Walk boldly and burn fiercely for Jesus. You are a force to be reckoned with. Never forget, he will always be with you and he'll always be for you.

Contents

Foreword by
T. D. Jakes Sr.

Imagine the sound of a stopwatch ticking. You have to imagine it because today the finest modern timepieces have absolutely no sound at all. Back in the day, you could easily hear the ticking of a watch. It reminded you of the brevity of life: how time flies and how valuable it really is, but more times than not, life is measured in increments of time that do not really quantify life's true value.

The sixty seconds in a minute, the sixty minutes in an hour, nor the twenty-four hours in a day, really capture the potency of that day. Thirty days in a month, twelve months in a year, and only God knows how many years are in each of our lifetimes. What I do know is that life is not a collection of years, days, or weeks. I've never sat by the bedside of an ailing loved one, a declining member, or an individual who has gone code blue and watched them recount how many days they have lived. They seldom count life in terms of weeks or years. The only things they really recall are the moments they had along the way.

Most people appreciate such moments in retrospect. They do so because hindsight is free of the clutter of the anxiety, complications, self-doubt, public perception, and all the other things that cloud our real-time view of great moments. Some of the most momentous moments in your life, marriage, career, or relationships are noted in their entirety after the event is over. Only a few of us know that our great moments are occurring while they are unfolding. Even fewer of us have the ability to prepare for the next great moment, sensing its arrival, anticipating its significance, and responding to it fully prepared by all the dismal days of normalcy that often surround those sacred spaces God allows us to walk into from time to time!

Instead, many find themselves wishing for another such moment to come along. There is nothing more remorseful than a lost opportunity to fill the soul with regret. Regret can be the first ingredient of bitterness, mixed with dashes of envy of others who did what we should have but for some reason failed to achieve.

Maybe that is why Pastor Sheryl is so tenaciously committed to awakening us to the power of each moment we experience. At the end of the day, seniors in nursing homes do not recall every day of their lives. Instead, they rehearse the moments. Photos capture them and enshrine them, archiving them as trophies that prove we had them. Those moments are priceless to them. They are the elixir of life itself. I have come to learn that there are great moments that define us, or in some cases, they are the moments that enrich our value or bankrupt our self-esteem.

I remember vividly the first time I met Pastor Sheryl. She was not a pastor at the time. She was an astounding worship leader. The moment we met, her husband, Joby, now the renowned Bishop Brady, and I would navigate a long-standing relationship that was laced with many more moments that would forge a clear bond. Sheryl's raspy deep throat, gut-wrenching, soul-stirring praise would fill a room with such power that even the most stoic person would find themselves on their knees in true heart-felt praise to God.

They would eventually travel with others and me around the country, singing and ministering in worship. They would do that until the next set of defining moments in her life would alter the course of us all. There were many moments of beautiful worship that affected us collectively and individually. I am sure there were personal moments and family moments that played into the destiny moments we all witnessed. As in my own life, one set of circumstances informs and imparts to the other.

Watching Sheryl lose her dear mother after having lost her sister was difficult. Nevertheless, I know that these moments affect us, reshape our thinking, mandate our focus, and alter what is most important to us all. Her ability to lead us into worship has morphed into an ability to guide us into unlocking God's purpose in every moment of our lives!

As I stand today and watch the continued growth, development, and the community impact of The Potter's House of North Dallas, where she now serves as Senior Pastor, I realize that while most people mark the upfront on-stage moments as catalysts that cause promotion, the reality is: all moments, both public and private, work together to shape the clay into the vessel God intends to use. Sheryl Brady has become a highly sought-after speaker. Her ministry has transcended denominations and organizations reaching far beyond our wildest dreams. She has ministered globally as well as nationally, sharing her faith, her fervor, and fire without wavering. People often think it is one defining moment that causes a career to soar, or a love relationship to ignite.

However, I understand that it isn't one moment but several moments that come together in tandem to accomplish God's purpose. Success is derived from fear and failure, tenacity and tears, purpose and passion, all working to ascertain God's strategies.

Gather all your experiences; they are the substratum of your life. Be careful to include the good, the bad, and the ugly. All of them are investors into the equity that affords you the strength and direction of your next destiny moment! As you turn each page of *Don't Miss the Moment*, allow your past moments to energize your steps forward to where the road is taking you. Untie yourself from being too overly absorbed into these current problems and complexities that distract so many of us. Instead, muster all your might to speak to your future and shout "Open the gates, I'm coming in!" It is when you read the words of people who have the scars from their cross and have earned the crowns in their careers to inspire you to overcome the tough times, that greatness breaks forth from the womb of your very being! I have a feeling that your greatest moments are ahead of you. If you have the faith to believe that too, then all I can say with her is "Don't Miss the Moment!"

Introduction

"I know the plans I have for you," declares the LORD, "plans to prosper you and not to harm you, plans to give you hope and a future. Then you will call on me and come and pray to me, and I will listen to you. You will seek me and find me when you seek me with all your heart."

Jeremiah 29:11–13

Uncertain anticipation gripped my stomach as we neared the security checkpoint at Lowell Correctional Institution just outside Orlando, Florida. I had been invited to minister to the women inside the maximum-security prison by a ministry friend who had herself been an inmate at that very penitentiary eight years earlier. My team and I were going to share the good news of the gospel with the prison's general population before meeting privately with five death-row inmates—the only women awaiting execution in the state of Florida.

You can never be sure what kind of atmosphere to

expect in a prison environment. And, as I surveyed the layers of razor-sharp barbed wire lining the towering perimeter fence, my pulse quickened. Our surroundings were intimidating to say the least, but God had orchestrated our visit so we might encourage, enlighten, and empower those prisoners—women he created in his image and loved with his whole heart. Our meeting would be but a small part of their extraordinary journeys; still I was honored that God had chosen me to bring his Word to them and I was determined to do my part well.

We made it through security without incident and followed a uniformed guard to the prison's chapel. As we neared, I could hear the faint but familiar melody of an old hymn. Gradually, music began to fill the air, and I was overcome by the sound of two hundred voices worshiping in unison. They sang and clapped with abandon to the King of kings. The Spirit was there; his presence was palpable. Every note carried with it a tenor of gratitude, every word a breath of release. These were women who had been found guilty in the eyes of the world, but blameless before Christ. And while their past mistakes had cost them their freedom, the Savior's sacrifice had bought them redemption.

Our escort led us around a corner, where we entered the sanctuary through a back door. When the women saw us, they stopped praising midstream to receive us with joyous shouts and thunderous applause. Unmistakably heartfelt, their warm welcome brought tears to my eyes.

I ministered to them with everything I had, from a place deep within, and they received the message I had prepared for them openly and readily. For two hours we laughed, cried, and glorified God. I was disappointed as my time with them drew to a close and we said our goodbyes.

Immediately afterward, we were led to the maximum-security wing of the prison. It was time to meet with the death-row inmates. I marveled at the carefully choreographed protocol followed by the staff and guards when moving these five women from one cell block to the next. The entire prison was put under lockdown. We were in the bowels of one of the securest buildings in the country, preparing to meet with five women who spend as many as twenty-three hours of every day locked away in solitary confinement. And it hit me. God had taken me to a place I had never been before.

I can still remember the sound the women made as they shuffled into the room single file, their shackled wrists and feet clanking rhythmically with each step. They sat down in the row of chairs across from me, silent but aglow. As their fellow inmates had been before them, those women were incredibly receptive to the gospel of Christ. For some months leading up to my visit, our host had been ministering to them from my book, *You Have It in You!* She also played for them weekly DVDs of my sermons at The Potter's House North. I was overcome with emotion as they all, one by one, expressed how my book and messages had pointed them to the truth of God's unending love, offered them hope in the midst of inconceivably trying circumstances, and grown them in their faith. Likewise, their insights and revelations blew me away, and their questions—outpourings of their desire to know God more deeply—provoked some of the most profound discussions I've ever had about the Lord, his ways, and our individual walks with him. And just when I thought I couldn't be more surprised about how God was working through these five women, they shared a story with me that to this day still moves me when I think about it.

The segregated section of the prison where death row is housed is also where prisoners who are sent to solitary confinement are located. As you can imagine, solitary confinement is typically reserved for inmates as a further punishment concerning their behavior while in prison. No books, no TV, nothing to keep one's mind occupied other than the four walls they are confined to. That alone could cause so much anxiety and stress on an individual. The ladies shared with me that on those days when someone was in close proximity in solitary confinement, they would lie down on the floor with their faces to the small opening in the door and read aloud excerpts of my book and workbook so that, in a very alone time, the other women could at least *hear* hope. Whew . . . that makes me want to lift my hands now and give God thanks for his redeeming power.

As I listened to five incredible stories of changed lives, God gave me a revelation of my own. Everything he had brought me through—all the trials, losses, lessons, and even victories—had prepared me for this moment. In a real-life illustration of Romans 8:28, he took all my mistakes and what appeared to be wasted steps and lost time and worked them together for my good.

By the world's standards, I had been destined to be nothing more than a failure, always coming up a day late and a dollar short. But God took me—a shy high school dropout whose story could have easily turned out so differently—and astounded me with a plan and a purpose I never saw coming. Statistically, if it had not been for his grace, I could have ended up on the other side of those prison bars. Instead he prepared me, often without warning and certainly without discussion, to do things I never dreamed of doing.

> Everything he had brought me through—all the trials, losses, lessons, and even victories—had prepared me for this moment.

— • —

Going from being single to being married can be traumatic for anyone, but especially for someone in her teens. I had only been on the planet for seventeen years before I made this dramatic life change. While most seventeen-year-olds are trying to discover who they are and what they will become, my narrative changed to one of trying to figure out who "we are" and what will "we become."

As a single young lady, I never had to worry about more grown-up responsibilities, such as paying bills, keeping a roof over my head and food on the table. Those were the fringe benefits of living in my parents' home. But, with the two little words "I do," the reality of adulthood suddenly set in. Your learning curve accelerates quickly when you attempt to flip the light switch on and find it's not working. Things like gas money, grocery money, and, the most important of them all, pantyhose money were nowhere to be found! The last of the three was particularly stressful to me. I remember one Sunday morning, while getting ready for church, when I realized just how much married life was costing me. I had my shoes, my dress, and my purse when I discovered that out of the two pairs of hose I had to my name, both had a run in one leg. So, being the creative person I am, I cut a leg out of each of them to make one working pair, because a girl's gotta do what a girl's gotta do.

Life continued to change rapidly for me. Seventeen months after our wedding, my husband and I welcomed our first daughter, Lana, into our world. We experienced the instant bliss that comes from the birth of a new child. I never knew I could love anyone like I loved her. This was love on another level. It was also stress on another level. Our sleeping patterns, or lack thereof, changed almost instantly. We now had to become experts on how to prepare bottles; change diapers; handle coughs, colds, and fevers; and navigate teething and the occasional temper tantrum. All this was amplified by the fact that we did not have room in our budget for any of it.

And just when I thought things couldn't get more chaotic in our newly formed family, when Lana was four months old, my husband informed me that he was quitting his job and we were going into full-time evangelistic ministry.

"Evangelistic ministry? Us? Is that where we go from city to city and hold several nights of revival?"

I had barely been out of Michigan! I mean, I had been an international traveler, in the sense that we were only two miles away from the Canadian border in Detroit and once in a while my friend Roberta would drive me through a tunnel to Windsor in Canada and then back over the Ambassador Bridge to the United States. Crossing the border was a lot easier back then. I didn't even need a passport. So I was, in a way, a global traveler. Outside of that, though, and the occasional summer vacation to my grandmother's house in rural Kentucky, I knew nothing about traveling.

Joining my husband to do ministry on the road was a brand-new experience for me. But, with Gladys Knight's lyrics echoing in my mind (*I'd rather live in his world than live without him in mine*) I did my part in packing up our car, our kid, and the few dollars of cash we had. And, just like that, our first ministry team was formed and we were on the road for Jesus. Though the whole experience was definitely different for me, I wouldn't trade it for anything. The lessons learned in this season of my life would stay with me forever. I didn't know it at the time, but this would become the catalyst that would propel me into a lifestyle God had prepared for me. A lifestyle of walking by faith and not by sight.

And, oh, what a lifestyle that was. Instead of sleeping in the comfort of my own home and my own bed, each night was, to put it mildly, an adventure. On the good nights when we had the resources to do so, we stayed in the most reasonably priced motel we could find. But I'm afraid those days, especially just starting out, were few and far between. Most of the time we stayed, as a lot of traveling evangelists did, in the local pastor's home, or the actual church. Do you know what it's like to be inside a church when everyone has gone home but you? I know it was my "Father's" house, but I sure liked it better when the rest of my family was there.

One room, in a particular church, resembled a cement-block fortress. Nothing warm or inviting about it at all. Just cold, rough cement blocks. And if the outside sounds bad, trust me, the inside was even worse. Upon entering the room, we discovered a single mattress lying in the middle of the concrete floor. For air-conditioning, we were allotted a single box fan that barely worked and, oh—did I mention that we were staying in Florida in the middle of the summer? I'll spare you the details, but for that story I have a hundred more that are equally terrifying.

On some church stops, the pastor would have us stay

in his home. This was always like playing the lottery for us, because you never really knew what you'd get. On so many occasions we stayed with some great families who took us in as their own. They loved on us, took care of us, and gave us a much-needed break from the stress of traveling. I'm grateful for the connections we made over the years. But on some occasions we ended up in insane situations. I will never forget this one house where our room was right next to the pastor's son's bedroom. The house was small with extremely thin walls. As we went to bed that evening, we were rudely awakened by the sound of acid rock. If you don't know what that is, imagine the loudest guitar in the world mixed with the lead singer screaming his head off over and over again. Not only could we not sleep because of the noise, I must say I was scared that the devil was sleeping right next to us. Without warning or announcement, we packed up and snuck right out the front door like thieves in the night!

If the living conditions weren't challenging enough, the food choices added even more difficulties. Like the glorious seven-day experience of roast beef. You guessed it, we stayed at one church who told us they would take care of all our meals with their hospitality team. *A hospitality team*, I thought. *Wow, this should be a great week!* Wrong! The truth is they *did* have a hospitality team that committed to cook for us daily, but failed to communicate about the menu with each other. As a result we were served roast beef . . . *every single day*! Now, don't get me wrong, we were grateful for a warm meal. And to be honest, I love leftovers. There's nothing like reheating yesterday's soup. But for seven days straight?! And roast beef? It's never really been one of my favorites. But we were on the road, serving Jesus, loving each other, and building a family, so I just went for it the best I could.

Even though you might think I'm crazy for saying I would never take away any of what I went through, I truly wouldn't. As strange as it sounds, I learned more about God in those unstable and uncertain times than probably any other point in my life. It was in those low moments while traveling that I discovered I served a God who was more than able to lift me out of them. When you get so low, sometimes you have no other direction to go but up.

Being on the road and having to depend on God built my faith day after day, week after week, and it ultimately took me to places I never could have gone into on my own. I mean, who gets to go into a maximum-security prison to share the gospel with women on death row and others who would eventually leave? What an absolute privilege! And when I walked into that prison that day, in with me walked all my experiences, frustrations of the past, hurts, rejections, victories, obstacles climbed, and lessons learned from a loving and caring Father.

I was able to preach hope that day because I knew what it was like to have hope deferred. I was able to encourage them not to allow being mistreated by others in their past to change who they were at the core. I was able to challenge them to see beyond the moment, because, even though I had stayed on cement floors, eaten the same food for seven days straight, and been tormented by acid rock, I was able to say, "Lord, I trust you that it won't always be like it is right now." And, believe me, it's one thing to say it; it's another thing to do it!

If we're going to really trust Him, we have to admit just how much we need Him. There's something about merging our *need* for God with the cry for help that moves Him on our behalf in an undeniable way.

Our testimony then becomes like that of the apostle Paul's: "Having therefore obtained help of God, I continue unto this day" (Acts 26:22 KJV). Because I had experienced that help on a personal level, I could now offer it to other women who were in front of me. Even though our journeys were different as well as difficult, the hope we could feel in the room that day was our common denominator.

Our early traveling days resulted in many people coming to know Christ, families restored, and lives changed. In this season, my husband and I learned to depend on each other and on God in ways we couldn't have imagined. In fact, many times when we were down to our last dime, people would stop us and sow financially into our ministry. Enough of those small, unexpected miracles happened along the way that I *knew* that God was faithfully sustaining us. He never failed no matter how hard it got and He gave me the grace to trust Him. And now, here I was, in Lowell Correctional Institution, sharing with, as well as being encouraged by, these incredible women. I never could have imagined that the culmination of all my steps would have led me to such a beautiful moment of ministry.

—— ◆ ——

When we look back on our lives, we can see so many purposeful moments that have been orchestrated by God, that lead to his plans for us. That, my friend, is the very essence of God moments. These moments are seminal snapshots in time—instances, circumstances, opportunities, trials, and revelations that have the potential to chart the course for everything they precede. Transformative in nature, they are bigger than the individuals to whom they are entrusted, and their repercussions often are as far-reaching as they are long-lasting. They require our deliberateness in order to reveal God's intentionality, and they work together for his glory and our highest good.

God moments are essential to everyone's life journey. We all experience them. Too often we miss, misinterpret, or even underestimate them, which plunges us into a cycle of frustration and fruitlessness. But they are there. They have your name on them. They belong to you and, like the pieces of a jigsaw puzzle, the whole picture will not be complete until they are recognized and set into their proper place.

Thankfully, all defining moments have defining characteristics. The purpose of this book is to help you both in recognizing them and acting on them as they occur. What good is it to simply see a moment and not seize it? Allow your spirit to be on high alert as we get started. Be open, honest, and objective with yourself so this book can be as helpful to your journey as possible.

Through these chapters, I want to help you prepare for moments, even the ones that seem impossible to obtain. I want to share with you how I've learned to wait—and wait the right way—when God has you in a "holding pattern." I want to show you how to confront your fears and go for it when going for it takes you into places you've never imagined you would go. Look for how God will surprise you with moments you had no idea were coming, as he's done for me time and time again. And even when rocky moments materialize along the way, I want to share with you some of the most painful moments in my life so you will know it's possible to stand through the roughest moments in yours.

> *Big moments are always made possible by small ones.*

And, most importantly, I want you to be aware that *big* moments are always made possible by *small* ones. Congratulations! You are experiencing a moment right now by reading this book. Thank you for giving me the privilege of helping you to master moments and not miss them!

chapter one

The Characteristics of Moments

I give the moments of my life over to You, Eternal One.

—Psalm 31:15 THE VOICE

"How did I get here?"

It's a question we often ask ourselves when we've hit bottom or when we've had an amazing success. Even though the journey up or the descent down isn't instantaneous, it can feel that way at times. It's easy to forget what eventually took us to the place where we stopped and realized we were someplace new.

If we think it over carefully, it's usually because of a variety of moments that came along, and the choices we made in those moments. Some were from God—opportunities he presented, like a clearly laid path he wanted us to follow. Others were manmade ideas—distractions from the prize or temptations to go down a less-than-healthy road. Whatever the case, we constantly face moments and make decisions in them.

For me, these moments often came in the form of small tests. Tests such as choosing to take the long road instead of a shortcut, building bridges when it would have been easier to burn them, always honoring other people, and giving God thanks in all things. Those were the little moments that led to many of the standout, memorable ones. How we manage the moments we are in will determine if we are ready for the moments that are yet to come.

Every major achievement, every vision realized, every ladder of success ascended—each one starts with a moment. And that early moment often doesn't seem like the stepping stone it is.

I believe most of us would attest that the old adage "When it rains it pours" has applied to us more times than we care to admit. We all know those seasons when our days are a continual downpour of one bad thing happening after another. Have you ever lived through a season where life has laid you out punch after punch, blow after blow? When everything that could go wrong did go wrong? We've all lived through moments such as these. One of those moments that stands out very clearly to me is when my family lived in Nashville. We had transitioned from traveling full-time to pastoring full-time. As with any new endeavor, we began with energy and excitement and a confidence that all would go according to plan. We felt God was on our side, so how could we fail?

How we manage the moments we are in will determine if we are ready for the moments that are yet to come.

It was a few days leading up to Easter, which, for anyone in ministry, is one of the most exciting days in a church. People wear their Sunday best, bring their families together, and celebrate the resurrection of Jesus. Spring shines brightly to showcase all its new growth, and new possibilities are in the air. It causes people to think afresh. Yet, despite what Easter should feel like, everything in our life at the time pointed in the opposite direction of resurrection.

Despite all our efforts, our church attendance was dwindling, which added emotional and financial strain on our family. On top of that, I was facing some very serious health challenges. After seeing my doctor, he'd recommended a procedure that would ultimately resolve my medical issue, but because we didn't have insurance it seemed impossible for me to obtain. I was physically sick, I was emotionally exhausted, and I was financially broke. My mind was a whirlwind of emotions.

One night I began my usual end-of-the-day prayer, but somewhere along the way my conversation with God began to go left. I was frustrated, angry, and confused. I had questions—actually more like demands—for God about things I would need in order to get through this season in my life. I laid out my list of demands as if in a hostage negotiation. I'm sure you've never talked to God this way, but I distinctly remember our tough conversation that night.

"I might as well be honest and tell you I don't even know if you are real!"

Let's face it. When you are in the midst of hard times, you start questioning even foundational things in your life. My faith was on edge, and I felt at the mercy of my circumstances.

I continued. "I need this surgery and don't know how I'm going to pay for it. My car needs work, and I don't know where to go to fix it. *And*, by the way, this Sunday is Easter. I would love to buy my three baby girls an Easter dress by tomorrow. I just need $100 dollars to do that, but God only knows where that would come from. (Pun intended.) Do you even care what is going on in my life? Do you know what I'm facing? Do you even know where I am?"

Needless to say, I was brutally honest with the one person who could take it without batting an eye.

I'm not someone who is overly spiritual about asking God for exactly what I want. I don't feel the need to pray for every single little thing in my life. For instance, I don't pray over what exact brand of corn God wants me to buy in the grocery store. Call me carnal, I guess! But, while prayer is the cornerstone to my walk with God, I was actually shocked that I said the things I said that night.

It's probably safe to say I just had a bad attitude, which provoked my honesty. But somehow, after listing my demands and feeling hopeless I found a way to fall asleep.

Early the next morning, I needed to drive my car to get it repaired. Still disgruntled, I said to God, "So, where should I go to get my car fixed?" I ended up taking it to a place I had passed on numerous occasions. I went in, explained my issue, gave them my keys, then made my way to the customer lounge to see how much this bill would further bust my budget. It was very quiet in that little room. There were no cell phones, no tablets, and no laptop computers at that time, so a waiting-room experience left you alone with your thoughts. In my case, being left alone with my thoughts could have been hazardous to my spiritual health. As I looked out the windows I noticed a McDonald's a few steps away from the car repair shop. And as clear as a bell, I heard God say, "Walk in that direction." I rattled off, still with a bad attitude, "I'm not hungry." Thankfully, he persisted. "Fine," I said, grabbing my purse and walking out the door.

I walked into the McDonald's, and ordered a soft drink, and quickly proceeded back to the repair shop. As I was just about to walk back in, I heard, "Go to the mall." Now my bad attitude, mixed with sarcasm, hit an all-time high.

"That's hilarious," I fired back. "It's only nine o'clock in the morning. Do you know that malls here on planet earth don't open until ten?" and "Why should I go to the mall when I don't have any money?" I want you to know that I normally don't have these in-depth conversations with God, but that day I did. Reluctantly, I took another three steps in the direction of the mall. And, as clear as ever, I then heard, "Stop! Look down under your right foot."

I looked down, and I was standing on a hundred-dollar bill. I could hardly believe my eyes! It was wrinkled, folded, and visibly worn, but to me it was the nicest, freshest, cleanest, most valuable hundred-dollar bill in the entire world. Without hesitation, I picked it up and started running as fast as I could toward the mall. With every step my joy and excitement was met with that inner voice of the Enemy trying his best to discredit what God had just done for me. I heard him try to convince me that it was fake and how embarrassed I would be when I couldn't use it. But I just kept running!

I arrived at the doors of the mall, still closed and locked because of the time, and looked long and hard at that hundred-dollar bill. It was as real as any hundred-dollar bill that had ever been printed! I kept looking at it and thanking God for the miracle that had just happened. But the real miracle, to me, was not that I was now able to get my three daughters new Easter dresses. Oh no, it was much bigger than that. The miracle was that God *knew where I was*!

He knew where I was physically, mentally, spiritually, financially, and emotionally. Despite my bad attitude and the sarcastic tone I'd had with him, he loved me enough to see past all of that and still showed me he was *with me* and *for me*. He literally ordered my steps. Psalm 119:133

came alive in me that day when, out of all the square footage in Nashville, Tennessee, he placed my right foot on the hundred-dollar bill I had prayed for just twelve hours earlier.

And the miracle I experienced that day never would have occurred had I not been willing to take those small yet significant steps! Each step, each decision, each instruction followed in the moment was a small, obedient act that combined with the next and culminated in an experience of his grace.

What Is a Moment?

Webster's dictionary defines a *moment* as "an indefinitely brief period of time; an instant." But moments can't be fully measured by seconds or minutes. Moments are specific, definite spaces where God works in a particular way. They are orchestrated by him!

Sometimes we don't realize the moments we're in until much later. After all, how can you recognize every instant of time? It's highly possible to never know the true value of a moment. Moments sometimes embody an intrinsic value we can't see. In fact, each one is woven into a grand tapestry that isn't finished until our last breath, the masterpiece that is God's plan for our lives.

As I look back over mine, I can see the way things have come together so beautifully as God surprised me again and again. There were pieces of my life I believed were good only for the cutting-room floor and never to be used again—fragments of failure, bad experiences, and poor decisions. Yet, like a skilled tailor, he merged my mess-ups with my successes. He salvaged the scraps, working them together to the point where I could no longer determine where one ended and the other began. His touch transformed what was marred and made it into something I could have never imagined.

And yet, the fear that follows failure still blocked my view of his plans for me for a good while. I was like a child clinging to the edge of the pool for dear life when all the while he was trying to show me how to swim and discover places far beyond the comfortable confines of the swimming pool. Despite all the things I felt were disqualifying me, he was still calling me out into those deeper, uncertain but beautiful waters. And his calling came in incremental stages that I like to call *God moments*.

The Defining and Seemingly Insignificant Moments

When I think back to the most memorable moments of my life, I am prone to reflect on the powerful ones. The ones that have proven to be catalysts. The ones that blew opportunities wide open, propelling me into places I could've never gotten to on my own. I'm talking about life-altering shifts where you are "here" one minute and "there" the next. Moments that have been marked with a sovereign signature, suggesting that no one but God could have accomplished what has been accomplished in your life. They are doors I walked through never again to return to what was: the moment I asked Jesus to be my personal Savior; the moment I said "I do" to my husband on our wedding day; the moment I heard my daughter Lana's cry, marking my first step into motherhood; the moment I was wheeled out of the hospital with Baby A "Tina" in one arm and Baby B "Nina" in the other, somehow knowing I had been given this double portion blessing *on* purpose *for* purpose; or the moment I acknowledged my call into ministry. The nine beautiful moments when my grandchildren came into the world and made their way into my heart. And the many moments that led to the final breaths of someone I loved more than my own self.

These moments define us. They are the ones we remember. But then there are the moments that aren't so recognizable, that we've probably even missed, that had the potential to be just as significant as the big moments, but were in fact extremely ordinary. The seemingly small and big moments both leave their marks on our history timeline.

Like an orchestra warming up, they can sound chaotic as they clash together. Yet with one wave of the conductor's hand, the chaos is quieted as each section harmonizes one with the other to produce a beautiful symphony. In our journey from birth to death, our moments are varied and complex, simple and mundane. Some seem to happen easily, and others seem carefully created. One thing is for sure: there are different types of moments.

We experience moments of

- beauty and betrayal,
- sickness and health,
- peace and unrest,
- success and failure,
- pleasure and pain,
- victory and defeat,
- calm and conflict,
- inspiration and frustration, and
- joy and sorrow.

Alone, some of these may seem insignificant, but nothing is truly insignificant. When they are pieced together, these moments become building blocks to something much greater than themselves. They are the entirety of who we are and what we are to become. The road that leads to our ultimate destiny is made up of our everyday steps, our daily routines, and the decisions we make in each moment, big and small.

Recognizing God Moments

All God moments have similar characteristics that make them recognizable. Here's a few to help you not misunderstand them when they manifest themselves in your life. Allow these to serve as signposts along your way.

1. They may be subtle.

We tend to operate under the misapprehension that God moments are rare occurrences that reveal themselves in grand fashion. We look for alarm bells, flashing lights, and neon signs that point to earthshaking revelations. But the truth is, God often speaks in whispers, strategically and incrementally unveiling his plans, preparations, and purposes through the most unassuming people and in the most unassuming ways.

Without question, Christ's birth—the long-awaited coming of the Messiah—was the world's greatest defining moment. Jesus, God's beloved and only son, whose rightful place is beside the almighty Father, humbled himself and became flesh so all men, without exclusion, would be cleansed of their sins and qualified to spend eternity in heaven with God.

Jesus was the stuff of legends. The prophets foretold his coming. The Jews believed he would herald a new era of world peace. Even the Sadducees and Pharisees awaited his advent. He was a true-life superhero, a long-anticipated champion come to save mankind. Never before and never since has there been a more significant moment than the Messiah's arrival.

And yet the world missed it. While everyone was

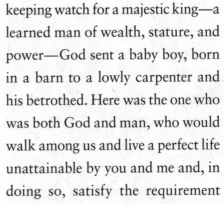

While all defining moments are momentous, not all defining moments are monumental.

keeping watch for a majestic king—a learned man of wealth, stature, and power—God sent a baby boy, born in a barn to a lowly carpenter and his betrothed. Here was the one who was both God and man, who would walk among us and live a perfect life unattainable by you and me and, in doing so, satisfy the requirement of a perfect sacrifice so that, in his death, he'd cover the punishment for our sin and deliver us from permanent separation from God (Rom. 6:23). But, because he didn't come in the package people expected, most of the world missed this moment.

You see, while all defining moments are momentous, not all defining moments are monumental. Don't miss what God has for you. Seek him everywhere and in everything, and you will be sure to find him.

2. They are costly.

God moments help shape our lives, but they also cost us because they require faith. And faith is hope in action. Many people make the mistake of approaching faith as a passive endeavor, believing that it begins and ends with hope, prayer, and waiting. Don't misunderstand me. Hope—desirous expectation—is a beautiful and important part of faith. And prayer is most certainly a necessary and powerful tool. Even waiting serves a purpose, as it produces patience, perseverance, and endurance. But it is action that activates God's promises for our lives. And, as we've talked about already, it's our actions, our decisions in each moment to say yes or no to God, that chart the course for our future. Saying yes to God can produce beautiful outcomes, but the initial yes itself can be anything but glamorous.

Often it involves relinquishing our most treasured plans, breaking our most stubborn habits, doing things we don't understand that seem slow, tedious, even painful. Because the work is tough and the payout is slow, many people lose hope and forfeit tomorrow's promises for today's platitudes. Dying to yourself daily is not easy; bearing your cross is not easy. And we often struggle to see how choosing the harder path of saying yes to God today is worth it for tomorrow. But it is. It always is.

When you realize what really matters, you'll give yourself to it no matter the cost. You can't afford to miss a moment because of a price you are unwilling to pay. Those who hold tight, push through, and press forward inevitably experience transformation that yields immeasurable rewards. Honor your moments through faith in action, and watch them give way to great accomplishments and even greater blessings.

3. They work underground and build our foundations.

A few years ago I read a story about the Chinese bamboo tree that I am pretty sure I will never forget! This particular tree starts out as a tiny little seed that must be planted, nurtured, and watered. In its first year, there are no signs of growth. In its second year, despite attentive and regular care from its owner, the seed still appears dormant. The third and fourth years yield more of the same—absolutely nothing—forcing even the most seasoned green thumb to wonder if all their labor has been in vain.

However, the fifth year—for those who remain dedicated and diligent—changes everything. The same seed that sat for years, dormant beneath the earth's surface, suddenly begins to sprout. As a matter of fact, by the sixth week of its fifth year, the Chinese bamboo tree grows eighty feet tall!

What appeared to be hopelessly dormant actually was growing the entire time; it simply was growing beneath the surface, in the places we could not see. This incredibly unique tree requires a strong foundation to sustain it as it matures. So, its first four years of life are dedicated to developing a root system deep enough and strong enough to support its potential for outward growth.[1]

In the same way, God rarely uses the moments of our lives the way we expect him to. While we wait restlessly for them to produce outward growth, God uses them strategically to promote inward change. As we face each moment and choose how we respond, we either allow God to build a strong foundation in our hearts for the future, or we don't. When we do, we take part in the slow and methodical work of God's transforming hand as he enriches us with his love, fortifies us in his truth, and matures us through his grace so we might be ready at the appointed time to receive all he has planned and purposed for us.

Saying yes to each of those moments makes you and me like the Chinese bamboo tree. Rooted in God, we pray ceaselessly, work tirelessly, and believe enduringly, investing everything we are and everything we have toward the cultivation of our destinies. There may be days of discouragement, moments of weariness when we feel like giving up and walking away, but we stand firm—our hope in God resolute! And, in response to our faithfulness, he preserves our potential and protects our possibilities, so that in due season we can spring forth in magnificent fashion—unshakable, unbreakable, and unstoppable.

Who Is in Control of Our Moments?

There's something in all of us that loves to be in control. From our earliest memories of school, we wanted to be the first in line, the first to answer a question, the first to be picked at recess. As adults we continue to strive for control of our time, our routines, our relationships, our careers, our lives, and everyone else's for that matter. All of us have control issues on some level. We think we can plot out our days, prioritize, and implement our schedules better than anyone. We believe our lives are ours to plan, to manage, and to shape as we wish. We want to know what, when, where, and how things are going to happen so we can guarantee the desired outcome. We go to great lengths to control our lives and our futures. We want to *map out* exactly how it should *turn out*.

But when our plan gets messed up, when an interruption changes our trajectory, when God doesn't show up when we expected him, or when our plans and dreams go astray, it can leave us distraught, disillusioned, and downright depleted.

"How did today go so wrong . . . this is not how I planned it at *all*!"

We might be angry, feeling sorry for ourselves, overwhelmed, and even confused.

This sense of being out of control makes us feel as if our moments *own us* instead of our owning them. Our demanding schedule requires us to miss an important family event. Everyone seems to need something from us. Or we feel like a victim of outside influences—a problem arises at work because someone else didn't do their job, resulting in our getting home late and missing out on the opportunity to tuck in our children, giving them that one last kiss on the cheek that lets them know we are their greatest fans!

No matter how well we plan and troubleshoot what *might* happen, the truth is, we are not the god of every moment of our lives. We do not own our moments, and they do not own us. Proverbs 19:21 says, "Many are the plans in a person's heart, but it is the LORD's purpose that prevails."

Think about it. Who owns your life? Is it you? Can you tell your heart to keep beating? Can you stop a natural disaster? Can you outrun or out-plan loss, failure, or heartbreak?

God owns our moments. We can't add to or subtract from the number of days we have. Only God can do that. Proverbs 9:11 says, "For by me thy days shall be multiplied, and the years of thy life shall be increased" (KJV).

Job 14:5 says, "A person's days are determined; you [God] have decreed the number of his months and have set limits he cannot exceed."

Our lives belong to God. And it is in those moments when things do not go exactly as we planned that we get to choose whether we say yes or no to his leading. How we respond tells us something about our hearts.

Early on in my life I learned the importance of surrender. Acknowledging Jesus Christ as my Savior was an easy decision for me. However, the longer I have walked with him on this journey, the more I have come to realize the difference between knowing him as my Savior and knowing him as my Lord. It was one thing to invite him into my heart, but putting him in charge of every aspect of my life was a completely different story!

Surrendering is something that has to take place on a daily basis for me, as each moment presents itself and I am given the opportunity to partner with whatever God is doing. And although complete surrender is contrary to our nature, sometimes it's a great relief to say, "It's all yours, God! I trust you. I'm watching for you. I'm listening for you. Please order my steps."

It's not always easy to let God be the author of our moments or the moments of those we love. In the autumn of 2017, my precious sister Kay was told she had six months to live. She'd already lived two years past the deadline the doctors gave her when she was first diagnosed. She grew worse by the day. We prayed fervently and asked prayer warriors around the globe to join us as we begged God for a miracle. I had complete confidence that God could heal Kay of the cancer that was eating her life away—if he chose to. I had seen him do miracles before, so why not now?

Kay was more than just a sister. She was a mentor, a confidante, a quiet coach whom I listened to more than anyone will ever know. She was a sounding board, a safe place that "Sheryl" the person could run to and find unconditional love! She was *for* me. She loved what I loved, cared about what I cared about, throwing the entire weight of who she was in God into everything I believed him for. There has never been nor will there ever be anyone like Kay in my life.

There were fifteen years between us. As a child, I always wanted to be wherever she was (and I have plenty of pictures to prove it). As an adult, however, she wanted to be near me, pouring every ounce of vision, ability, knowledge, wisdom, and passion she possessed into making sure that I would see everything God had promised me come to pass. Seeing her body wither away left me full of fear and devastation and, to be honest, sometimes infuriated. Her life didn't feel finished on this earth to me. She had much more to give, and we needed her here.

But God's ways are not my ways, and little by little she was leaving us.

In the same year that Kay was making her exit, my twin grandchildren, Mason and Mariah (my "M&M's"), were making their arrival. It was the best of times and the worst of times. I was watching the Lord *give* and *take away* all at the same time. In the many moments before Kay's last breath, I wondered what God was doing. Still to this day I wonder why he did what he did. The truth is, I may never know. But God knows my days, and he knew Kay's. Rest assured, he knows yours too. He has a plan bigger than our years upon this earth, and each moment of our lives is loaded with purpose and intention. Although I wish I could wrap this part of my life up in a pretty little bow and say I know exactly what God was doing in those wrenching moments, I can't. But the one thing I do know is that he has been a bright light in the darkest places of my life. Whether we see him or not, we *know* he is near and he is at work.

God may not show us everything on the road ahead. He may not say yes to all our prayers. He might not answer our questions in this life. But he will give us what we need to go the distance, to run the race well. His Spirit will be our companion and our comfort. He promises to hold our hands or carry us through the days that are hard, even as he does the quiet work of developing our roots and shaping our hearts and preparing us for what is yet to come. In the middle of all that, he is there, always there.

Being Aware in the Moment

I often think about the moments the disciples spent with Jesus. I wonder if they caught even a little of the miracle and weight of them. Did they stop to really look at what Jesus drew in the dust with his finger? When Jesus raised the little girl from the dead, did they look to see if he wept or smiled? Did they study how his hands moved when he washed their feet?

They experienced so many beautiful moments that must have felt risky, overwhelming, confusing, and life-changing. I wonder if they could imagine what these moments meant in the light of the future for all believers.

Jesus still has the power to overwhelm our hearts with moments—moments that change us and moments that can change the world. They may not seem essential at the time, but let's not ever underestimate them because moments are powerful. I've heard it said like this: "They are small enough to miss but big enough to change our lives forever."

Just as the disciples couldn't imagine we would be reading about their moments all these generations later, studying them, imagining them, neither can we imagine how the moments God brings to us now might impact the future.

You and I are integral parts of an intricate plan—a divinely orchestrated strategy set in motion before the earth was conceived. Like winding roads on a map, we are sovereignly interconnected—past, present, and future intersecting in accordance with his will not only for our individual lives but for humanity as a whole. History is rich with examples of people unwittingly groomed by and used of God to achieve his perfect end.

Joseph, a young nomad, sold into slavery by his own brothers, had no way of knowing that their betrayal was a sanctioned part of God's plan to save an entire nation. Nor did Abraham Lincoln, a self-educated man of humble circumstance who dismissively referred to himself as "a floating piece of driftwood," know that he would some-day become a leader used by God to turn the tide of slavery in America.

Thankfully, knowing who we are *in him* is not a pre-requisite for becoming who we're called to be *through him*. Don't get me wrong: sometimes God allows us to witness his plan unfold layer by layer, and he grants us the grace to understand the true magnitude of his hand while it is at work in our lives. But many times, we are unwitting participants of a predestined plan set in motion long before we existed with a resolution that will not be realized until long after we're gone. Either way, we are all—each and every one of us—handcrafted and tailor-made by God for a purpose greater than ourselves.

God moments introduce you to people, expose you to opportunities, and create circumstances that continually steer and usher you toward your ultimate destiny and the fulfillment of God's grander design. At their onset, the moments may seem overwhelming. Often, they thrust you into uncharted, ever-enlarging territories that can leave you feeling lost and forgotten. In certain seasons, they can even make you question your capacity and level of preparedness. Though you may not always believe it or perceive it, know that you are here by divine design. You are an irreplaceable part of an irrevocable plan; God picked and equipped you according to his absolute knowledge in order that you might accomplish his perfect will.

Remember that God has a destiny mapped out for you, and it's in the daily steps, following the path of his moments, where your purpose is discovered. Grab this moment, and prepare to start seeing. Remember, God moments are all around you, all the time, in the people you meet, in the challenges you face, and in the simple victories that lead to great success.

chapter two

Preparing for
the Moment

We're friends, right? I mean, we've spent an introduction and one whole chapter together already, so basically that equals friendship. And because of that friendship I can be honest about something. I'm just going to come right out and say it. Here goes.

I'm not into sports at all!

There. I said it. Whew . . . I feel so much better.

I know there are times I might preach in a Dallas Cowboys jersey during the Super Bowl. There are also times I might post a picture of me with some signed Steph Curry shoes that were given to my husband around the NBA playoffs, but really that's about it. I'm just not into sports.

My husband, however, is a completely different story. He can sit for hours in front of the TV watching sports. We have parties dedicated just to them. His Super Bowl parties are legendary, filled with decor, food, lots of people, food, and more food. When the NBA season starts, all the way through the Finals, he can be heard yelling at the TV while his beloved Golden State Warriors are playing. You would think he's sitting courtside in Oakland. He *loves* it, and I love that he loves it so much. But not me. Not me at all.

For someone who cares so little about sports, it's funny that watching a sport showed me something so powerful. Many years ago, I took a walk on a long pier on the West Coast. As we got farther and farther I started noticing people lying on surfboards and bobbing up and down in the ocean. I marveled at how long they just stayed in the water waiting for a wave to ride. But not just any wave— the right wave. Wave after wave would pass. Some seemed larger than others and, to the naked eye, like perfectly good waves. Yet these seasoned surfers waited patiently; they knew what they were waiting for. Then, at just the right moment, these patient surfers would see it, swim out ahead of the break, jump up on their boards, and ride the wave they had waited so long for all the way to the shore.

I learned so much that day about how important it is to be prepared to ride the waves. In fact, I'm going to make a statement I hope you can believe and adopt for your own life: waves of opportunity are being presented to us almost every day. It's true. Just because we don't recognize an opportunity doesn't mean it's not there. It's like the wind Jesus describes in John 3:8, that "blows wherever it pleases. You hear its sound but you cannot tell where it comes from or where it is going."

> Just because we don't recognize an opportunity doesn't mean it's not there.

I believe God has opportunities waiting for us on a daily basis, but so often we aren't prepared to ride them in the way he intended. So we miss them. But we don't have to. We can be like those surfers, watching for them and waiting for them, ready to go when God presents them to us. So what does that look like? How does one prepare to ride something that is visible but invisible at the same time? In hindsight I've discovered a few principles that I know to be true. They have, on many occasions, prepared me for and propelled me to the God moments in my life. My hope is that by sharing a few of them with you, you may be able to do the same.

To Know His Way, We Must First Adopt His Heart

One of the many reasons I'm so glad Jesus is in my life is that when I accepted him to be Lord, I accepted his nature in place of my own. A primary belief in the Christian faith is that human beings are sinful in nature. We are born that way, needing redemption, needing a Savior. If I left it up to my own way of doing things, it would be instinctive for me to react in a way that's not in line with the nature of Christ.

For instance, to some people, when served an injustice, the first inclination is to retaliate in kind with the same measure, or even greater. Insult produces insult; pain produces pain. It is a fact that hurting people hurt people. The cycle continues until we feel we've somehow broken even with the offender. But the more I spend time with God and in his Word, the more I begin to understand that by identifying myself as a follower of Christ, I no longer have the right or even the option of operating in an eye-for-an-eye mentality. The old saying is true: "An eye for an eye makes everyone blind." Trust me, nobody ever wins with this type of mind-set. Through our faith in Jesus Christ, we are new creatures, which, at its core, means old patterns must break and new ones must be established. I must reboot the hard drive of my life and say yes to a new way of thinking, acting, and even reacting. This is what opens the door to knowing God more deeply and seeing how he's at work as those opportunities to partner with him become more apparent.

One of my favorite scriptures is Psalm 24:3–4, which says, "Who, then, ascends into the presence of the Lord? And who has the privilege of entering into God's Holy Place? Those who are clean—whose works and ways are pure, whose hearts are . . . sealed by the truth, those who never deceive, whose words are sure" (TPT). Wow . . . talk about a high standard! If you really dig into what this passage is saying, you will find it is discriminatory! It's not for everybody. Please don't misunderstand me. Our salvation is a free gift from God. That's settled. But what I want you to be aware of is that there are places, levels to ascend to in God, that are available only to those who will pay the price of admission. It is costly.

We are called to be pure, to operate out of God's truth. But what does it mean to have pure hearts that choose truth? It means we let go of our natural tendencies and embrace God's way. We extend grace in places it was never extended to us. We choose forgiveness when unforgiveness would be so much easier. We allow love to eclipse hate. And if you think love is an easy emotional *feeling*, it certainly is not! It is a decision. It can be hard and tedious work. It requires patience, kindness, choosing not to envy, being humble when you want to be proud. Love doesn't parade itself; it doesn't advertise itself. It doesn't exalt or exhibit itself. It is not overinflated. It is not arrogant. It doesn't act superior. Love prefers and always shows honor. What's easy about any of that?

Having this kind of a changed heart, a renewed nature, is risky. It's a picture of Hosea loving his unfaithful wife, Gomer, because real love reaches around, apprehends unfaithfulness, and chooses to love anyway. It's personified in King David caring for the lame son of his late friend, Jonathan (2 Sam. 9). When we love others, there's never a promise that we will be fully compensated, and yet love loves anyway. Love's way is counterintuitive to our normal, everyday, selfish nature that has been wired in us from birth. Love's way will have you wrestling with yourself late at night, because you know that what you *want* to do is not what you *should* do.

Love's way washes you of every unclean motive; it purifies your heart. And, in doing so, love's way sets you up to see God more clearly, because "only the pure in heart can see God" (Matt. 5:8, paraphrased). To *see* God is to see what he's doing, how he's working behind the scenes, what he's positioning you for, so you can seize the opportunity he places in front of you and catch your next wave.

Preparation Starts with *Pre*

In the mid- to late-nineties we were just starting to see the emergence of modern technology as we know it. Computers had been out for a while, and we were getting more and more accustomed to the internet being a part of our daily lives. Around 1996 I found myself ministering around the world almost more than I was at home. To help us better manage the speaking invitations, we requested all inquiries be submitted through a modern-day miracle called a fax machine. That's right, the good ole fax machine. If you don't know what that is, google it!

In addition to the fax machine, my staff had investigated and started implementing a new website, which had features like online prayer requests, ways to contact our ministry, and this new thing called an online store. Long before the days of Amazon Prime, an online store was a fringe way of looking at commerce. I still remember the apprehension I had about this, as well as that of some of my ministry peers who were thinking about investing in this type of technology. Who would feel safe enough to put their credit card information on a computer screen, send you their money, and hope you would get it and ship them their favorite CD or DVD? (If you need to know what those are, google them too!) But, after a series of meetings and discussions, I decided to give this new online store a chance.

For a couple of months, we worked hand in hand with programmers to develop it. To be honest, I started regretting my decision as soon as I began counting the cost of creating it. It seemed like every week the staff were coming to me, saying, "We need more money for this," or "We forgot to add this." I felt like resources were just leaving our bank account for something that seemed like a questionable idea in the first place.

Eventually, after three months of work and a few thousand dollars spent, we launched our sherylbrady.com website with an all-new dedicated online store. We were so proud of it. I can see the purple and black colors of it now. We launched it and then waited for the big return.

One month passed, and not much happened.

Another month, and another. I thought, *Well, at least it looks nice.*

Then I got an invitation to minister at the TBN studios in Nashville, Tennessee. It was one of the first times I'd had an opportunity to speak to such a large audience through the medium of television. I was excited and a bit nervous. A few of my family made the trip with me to the taping. We were going to give it our best shot with the help of God on my side. Looking back now, I laugh at how the night unfolded. Let's just say things didn't go exactly as planned.

As I took the stage, I recalled something Bishop T. D. Jakes had taught me. He'd said, "Sheryl, when you get opportunities like this for TV, always stay within the time limit they give you. If they say twenty minutes, don't do nineteen and don't do twenty-one. Stay on that tightrope of time, and walk it until you get to the end of it." So that's what I was prepared to do. Stay in my time. No more, no less!

I preached my heart out that night. Through my message I kept a watchful eye on the large cue card they would bring to the side of the stage to keep me on track. I remember the first sign said, "Twenty minutes," and then the second, which seemingly came out five minutes later, said, "Five minutes left." *Five minutes?* I thought. I felt like I'd barely just begun. Time must have *flown by.* I started to exit out of my message, to close out my time.

But, as I glanced to the side of the stage, the cue card magically turned to ten minutes. *Wait . . . how did we go from twenty to five and back to ten?* I later found out that the cue card specialist had inadvertently held up the wrong card in the beginning. When I really had fifteen minutes, I thought I'd only had five. Despite my confusion, I had to figure out what to do next as I'd already closed my message.

My instincts kicked in, and I just did what I know how to do best: "Lift your hands, and give God a praise in this building."

I can only imagine what my son-in-law Chris was thinking as he sat behind the keyboard that night. He had a profound way of marrying his gift of music to my gift of ministering the Word, and we'd always had great chemistry together, moving rhythmically as if we were in a dance. Except this night his dance partner seemed to have two left feet. But, like he always does, he found a way to tap into the flow of the evening, and off we went.

We worshiped our hearts out for that last ten minutes, and God moved in the room. I stuck to my twenty minutes and walked away grateful that God had given me an opportunity to serve his people once again. Case closed, let's go home!

It was not until we arrived back in North Carolina that my staff started telling me all the good that had come from that television appearance. We'd received enough orders to pay for the monthly maintenance of the site, dozens of invitations to speak, and hundreds of prayer requests. People had poured their hearts out to us and asked us to agree with them for miracles. Many of them said, "We had never heard of you before tonight, and God used you to speak hope to our situation." The amount of support we received through the website was overwhelming. All of a sudden, it seemed our investment in that new piece of technology was a great thing after all. And if we hadn't gone through the early days of setting it up, we might have come up short when the responses flooded in. It was another example of God showing me that the most important part of preparation is the "*pre*." It almost always happens before.

It's often too late to try to get things in order when the opportunity presents itself. The many months and many dollars we'd spent were in preparation for the wave that was heading my way. Not only were the people who tuned in that night blessed, but that moment maximized into full-blown opportunities. It was as if my opportunities had opportunities. Why? Because I prepared in advance! But isn't that what faith is all about? Doing something before we see any evidence of it? Hebrews 11:1 tells us, "Faith is the substance of things hoped for, the evidence of things not seen" (KJV). It's Noah building an ark when they had never even experienced rain. It's Abraham going to a land he knew nothing about, because God told him it was his inheritance. It's Joshua marching around Jericho for seven days with no evidence anything would happen . . . until it did!

I had no idea my investment into that website would play such a major role in ministering to people's lives over the years. Our website has evolved so many times since we first launched it. It helped our ministry turn the corner of technology that allowed us to venture into other digital mediums to reach even more people with the gospel. From a website we moved to a Myspace page (google that too). From Myspace to Facebook, Twitter, YouTube, and Instagram. We've literally seen people from all over the world be ministered to through social media. They've helped connect us with people just like you. You may even be reading this book as a result of them. It was God's positioning us through our preparation for what was next.

Could it be that your lack of preparation is the holdup in the next big thing God wants to do in your life? Could it be that you could make one move that would cause God to open the windows of heaven? Destiny doesn't happen in spite of us; it happens because of us. There are things you and I must do to provoke the release of God-given moments in our lives. What moments are you missing because you haven't prepared for them?

Not Every Wave Is Your Wave

So now that you're motivated and ready to jump on the next wave God is sending your way, I do need to caution you that not every wave is for you. When I think back to my revelation on that pier, I remember how long those surfers just lay there on their boards. Wave after wave came, but they did nothing. Didn't move at all. They just waited. A few times some of them would start the motion of swimming out to attempt to ride but quickly stopped when they realized it just wasn't the right wave.

Think about this for a moment: not every wave belongs to you. It's a powerful concept I use in my own life to give myself permission to just say no to certain things. It's a delicate tightrope to walk at times, because when you are not accustomed to opportunities coming your way, you feel as though you can't afford to say no to any of them. The last thing on earth you would ever want to be perceived as is ungrateful. So, as a result, you open every door, accept every invitation, and take on every task because it initially feels like a blessing. And don't get me wrong, it is always an honor for people to make room for you. But I can tell you through firsthand experience that sometimes what starts out as a blessing can leave you feeling "weary in well doing." We eventually begin to realize that by taking on *everything*, we will inevitably find ourselves exhausted, with little strength or passion left for *anything*.

Extra, extra, read all about it—the sooner you learn that every door is not a God door, the more prepared you will be for the ones that are. Good opportunities do not always equate to God opportunities. Unlike God, we are a limited resource, and if we are not careful we will find ourselves in the trap of overcommitment. There is nothing worse than finding out you have an overdrawn account with a negative balance. I'm not limiting that to a bank account located in a building on the corner where you conduct your financial transactions. I'm also referring to the many bank accounts we must manage in the inner chamber of who we are, such as our faith, peace, compassion, relationship, and love banks. Please trust me when I tell you that when you spend yourself in places that matter the least, it will cost you in places that matter the most. Being prepared to differentiate between what matters and what doesn't, what is *good* and what is *God*, is vital to managing the success he wants to send in your direction.

An important thing to remember is that the timing of God and the grace of God go together. Anything we do outside of his timing is something we don't have the grace for, and anything we do outside of grace is usually exhausting and fruitless. Meaning we will have no harvest to show for our labor. A great indicator that you are in God's timing and surrounded by his grace is fruit. Being fruitful should be the heartbeat of every believer. In fact, it's one of the first commands God gave to man. The very first words he ever spoke to Adam were, "Be fruitful, and multiply" (Gen. 1:22 KJV). Nothing about this is a suggestion. God expects us to bear fruit. Not only fruit, but *more* fruit, and *much* fruit. He himself is a God of more than enough, and if we are his children, made in his likeness and his image, then we too should be mindful of his desire for us to bear "much fruit."

> Good opportunities do not always equate to God opportunities.

There is a difference between being busy and being fruitful. If we're not careful, we can become so busy being "busy" that we fail at being fruitful. We sacrifice the calling we have in different areas of life to chase the opportunity that wasn't God's best for us in the first place. There is a wave, an opportunity, an open door, a blessing, and a bountiful harvest that has your name on it. Don't miss it by making the mistake of failing to be prepared for it.

So how do we make the distinction between better and best, great and greater, good and God? It really isn't all that difficult if you know the proper pattern to follow. Let's look at a few tried-and-true ways that have always worked for me.

Knowing God

Your relationship with God will ultimately be your best and most effective way of recognizing your waves. The book of Daniel says it like this: "But the people that do know their God shall be strong, and do exploits" (KJV). It's a no-brainer for me that I want to spend my time with the one who already has my life planned out. Having a relationship with God allows you to understand him clearly when he gives you the green light to proceed or the red light to stop. You can't receive anything from someone you don't allow to speak in your life. Spending time with him gives him the opportunity to speak into you.

Prayer still works. Talking to God still matters. Listening for God's direction is still important. Don't make the mistake of thinking that prayer is strictly a monologue, because it is not. It's most definitely a dialogue. It's where you talk to him and he talks to you. So many times in my life, I've felt the nudge of the Holy Spirit not to do something and I've simply made the decision not to do it. Some call it a feeling in their gut; I call it feeling it in my spirit.

God can talk you through whatever you may be facing in life. He is the ultimate communicator. Unlike us, he's never at a loss for words. He will speak to us through ways unimaginable. He speaks to us through the smile of a friend, the kindness of a stranger, and the simplicity of a child. He speaks purpose through the dawning of a new day and peaceful rest at the setting of the sun. He speaks through a soft touch in a painful place, as direction in the midst of distraction, and a voice of clarity in the time of confusion. We serve a speaking God. He can speak through anything and everything. He speaks through his creation, he speaks through his voice, he speaks through his Word, which is a lamp unto my feet and a light unto my path (Ps. 119:105). His Word illuminates where we should put our feet next with assurance and confidence. When we make the investment to listen, God will make the investment to speak. And don't panic in those times when it feels as though God is silent. When you can't hear his voice, look to what he has written in his Word.

Knowing Others

Often our life's decisions are paralleled by our life's associations. When is the last time you took inventory of those you surround yourself with? Do you have people in your life who have been places you want to go, have embraced God-things you are still reaching for, or have succeeded in areas you have yet to succeed in? Do you have anyone in your life who will tell you the truth? Because honesty really is your best friend. Do you have at least one person who will just listen to you no matter what? Who is not there to fix *it* or *you* but is just your sounding board?

Having the right people around us bridges the gap between our strengths and our weaknesses. There is a reason God said, "It is not good for man to be alone."

Knowing Ourselves

While it's important to know those who surround us, it's even more important that we know ourselves. What makes you tick? What makes you happy or sad? What brings you fulfillment? What drives you? What depletes you? What calms you or leaves you anxious? Knowing yourself is so important for knowing the types of waves you should swim out to ride. It gives your spirit the green light when an opportunity presents itself, because you have already run it through the internal processes of asking, "Will this bring me fulfillment, will I have passion to complete it, and can I have *fun* while in the process?"

When you realize that you were born *on purpose, for*

purpose you understand that God has wired and equipped you with everything you need to fulfill that specific purpose. It's your calling and your assignment that gives you your edge, your lane, and your highest and best use. It's where you fit and where you are the most fruitful. Any time you step outside of that it leaves you with a sense of failure and frustration, and you'll know you've jumped on a wave that is not yours to ride.

Overcoming the Anxiety of Identifying Your Wave

Have you noticed that people are fighting anxiety today more than ever? Perhaps it's been there all along, but with the rise in popularity of social media we're more aware of it. We're anxious over where we are in life or where we are not. People have anxiety over career choices, wardrobes, cars, homes—you name it and we are anxious about it. We're anxious to get *all* these things resolved as quickly as possible. Patience goes out the window when we are anxious. Waiting on the Lord is obsolete when we are anxious. We find ourselves fighting the internal voices that remind us we will never measure up, never be enough, never win at anything. And we are especially anxious when we're trying to figure out whether the opportunity in front of us is what God has for us or simply a distraction from our destiny.

Although the concept of anxiety may be new for

some, it is no surprise to God at all. He knew all along that we would wrestle with the demon of anxiety. Paul admonished us in his letter in Philippians,

> Don't be pulled in different directions or worried about a thing. Be saturated in prayer throughout each day, offering your faith-filled requests before God with overflowing gratitude. Tell him every detail of your life, then God's wonderful peace that transcends human understanding, will make the answers known to you through Jesus Christ. (4:6–7 TPT)

Notice a few points there:

- Do not be anxious for *anything.*
- Pray over *everything.*
- Give thanks in *all things.*

As a result, God will give you peace and make his answers known to you. Following Paul's example will keep anxiety at bay, even as we feel worried and pulled in different directions. Keep your focus on trusting God, continually coming back to prayer, and having a thankful heart, and you'll find peace even as you wait for your moment.

Believe me when I tell you that waves of opportunity are coming your way. Prepare to catch the ones that belong to you, allowing them to carry you to places you could have only imagined you would be.

chapter three

Waiting on the Moment

In the summer of 1929, a seventeen-year-old girl named Minka believed her heart might shatter into pieces as she said goodbye to her baby girl. Minka knew it was best that her daughter be given to a good adoptive home. This was the Depression-era Midwest. Minka had only an eighth-grade education, she lived with her mother and stepfather on a farm in South Dakota, and, worst of all, her baby's father was unknown because her precious child had been conceived through rape.

Minka had believed babies were delivered by stork until she and a friend were assaulted by two men while on a walk in the woods. She never saw the man again. But what would people think of her baby if they knew? What kind of life could she have with a single mom with little hope for a future?

With the help of her mother, stepfather, and their kind pastor, Minka moved to the Lutheran House of Mercy to wait for her baby to be born and say goodbye. The problem was that when the time came, Minka fell helplessly in love with the baby she named Betty Jane. But Minka sacrificed her heart so her daughter could have a better life. She never got over the loss. She wrote letters to the House of Mercy inquiring about any bit of news about her daughter for the next twenty years. She also prayed. She prayed for Betty Jane year after year, especially on May 22, her birthday. Minka would pull out the lone photograph she possessed, and she'd say a special birthday prayer. This went on for seventy-seven years.

On May 22, 2006, ninety-four-year-old Minka prayed a different prayer. For the very first time in nearly eight decades, Minka didn't just pray for Betty Jane. She also made a request: "Lord, if you would just let me see her, I promise you I will never bother her."

As Minka prayed, she felt at peace, but nothing seemed to happen. She put away the photograph for another year and returned to her life in Southern California where she folded the weekly church program and often had Bible study in her own little apartment. Minka had married in the years after giving up her baby. She'd raised two more children, watched grandchildren grow up, and had buried all the people she'd known while growing up.

But halfway across the country, God set things in motion. Her "Betty Jane" was now seventy-seven-year-old Ruth Lee, and on that same day, her birthday, a 270-page packet arrived in her mailbox revealing the origins of her birth and including copies of the letters Minka had written to the House of Mercy over the first twenty years of Ruth's life.

A few weeks later, Minka received a phone call from a man inquiring about her. Minka suspected identity theft, until he introduced himself as her grandson and asked, "Would you like to talk to your Betty Jane?"

After seventy-seven years of waiting, Minka was speaking to her daughter. Soon after, she wrapped her arms around her Betty Jane once again.

There are moments in our lives when God calls us to wait.

We may be praying for a spouse, or a child, or a new home, or a better job. We might feel anxious that our lives aren't where we thought they'd be by the time we thought they'd be. We might believe our progress is being hindered by circumstance, by an illness, by a dead-end relationship, or by a boss who can't see our value. We might want everything to change . . . now.

And why wouldn't it change? There are many references throughout Scripture to how God works things together for our good, how he has bigger plans in mind than our own, and how he will direct our steps. We have faith that God is on our side, so he should see our logic and support our plan, right? But, still, nothing is happening. Doors aren't opening. No one is cooperating. Nothing is working. In moments like this, it would do us good to remember that just because he doesn't answer us when we want him to does not mean he is denying our requests. It may simply be a matter of timing. It may be that God's answer is, "Wait."

The Discipline of Patience

Patience during times of waiting can be one of the most difficult of disciplines.

Like restless children on a road trip, over and over again we ask the question, "Are we there yet?" *Just how much longer will we have to sit still? How much longer will we need to wait? Where is the end of this seemingly endless line I've found myself in? Is it just ahead, around the block, or could it possibly be years down the road?*

All the unknowns associated with waiting can leave us terribly uncomfortable. It may even feel as though God is asleep behind the wheel. Or, worse than that, waiting can often leave us feeling like the God who said he would "never leave us" has all but abandoned us. It is mind-blowing to me just how quiet God can be while we are waiting.

Outward waiting can often produce inward struggles that leave us feeling delayed, denied, unsure, and unproductive. However, whether we see it or not, we have to trust that even in times of waiting God is steadily at work in our lives. Whenever we pray and ask him to deliver us from something yet he chooses to keep us *in it*, it just means he is going to bless us more from being in it than he would by bringing us out of it.

Someone reading this book today needs to know that when our hearts are positioned properly in seasons of waiting, not one moment will be wasted. Every promise God has made you, every dream he has given you, and every vision he has shown you is coming! It will come, it shall come, and it must come. And when you least expect it, those of you who have been on the sidelines and in the background will be ushered from behind the scenes and placed center stage. And as the curtain rises, everyone will know that you have passed the test of waiting. Be patient, and rest assured that life is moving in your favor underneath what appears to be still and unbothered waters. Cry if you must, but remind yourself that every crying season has an expiration date: "Weeping may endure for a night, but joy comes in the morning" (Ps. 30:5 NKJV).

Right now, think about a gorgeous blue lake with a smooth-as-glass surface reflecting a cloudless blue sky. Across the lake's surface, it seems as if nothing is happening. Not one movement or ripple. But imagine dipping down below the surface. That lake is alive and filled with various kinds of fish, turtles, plants, maybe a sunken rowboat, a boot, a tire, a fishing pole. From our view at the shoreline, we can never see what is going on under the surface. It's the same during moments of waiting. God is doing something. We just can't always see it.

> We may feel stuck in a moment we don't want, but that moment is doing something in us we can't see.

James 1:4 says, "Let patience have its perfect work, that you may be perfect and complete, lacking nothing" (NKJV). Other Bible versions translates "patience" as: "let perseverance finish its work" (NIV) and "when your endurance is fully developed" (NLT).

Patience has a purpose. It perfects you, matures you, and strengthens your character. These times appear stagnant, but rest assured there is more to the moment than meets the eye.

> Consider it a sheer gift, friends, when tests and challenges come at you from all sides. You know that under pressure, your faith-life is forced into the open and shows its true colors. So don't try to get out of anything prematurely. Let it do its work so you become mature and well-developed, not deficient in any way. (James 1:2–4 THE MESSAGE)

We may feel stuck in a moment we don't want, but that moment is doing something in us we can't see. Be patient, go through it, wait for God to move you at his pace and when he's ready. Even if it means he chooses to take you down the long road.

The Importance of the Long Road

Over the years, I've learned many of life's greatest lessons by taking what I call the long road. Often we want our life to mirror the way we navigate to destinations through our GPS. We simply punch in an address and choose the fastest route. But there's so much I've learned about God's faithfulness and God's timing that could only have been found by taking the long road.

I wouldn't be who I am had I taken the shortcuts in life. There are significant relationships I would have never built, lessons I would have never learned, and adventures I would have never embarked on if I'd taken a shorter route. It's taken every step on the long road to sustain me for every life experience I would face.

The long road exposes us to more, broadens our experiences, and positions us to capture many moments we would have otherwise missed. It gives us a greater sense of appreciation, because we understand what it took to get us there. We are often like children who fail to fully value certain things because we cannot comprehend the cost. Whether it's a meal out as a family, waking up in warm, safe beds, or taking the dream vacation to Disneyland, children (typically) have no idea what this costs in time, money, and commitment. In the same manner, if we don't evaluate what something really costs us, we may have the tendency not to recognize its worth.

After waiting, being patient, and growing through life's challenges, it is the lessons we've learned along the way that give us a greater appreciation for the journey.

One of the hidden treasures that can often be found on the long road is the gift of longevity. Shooting stars may give us a brilliant show of lights, but everyone knows they fall just as fast as they rise. Why? Because they haven't developed what is needed for sustainability. Long-term ascension can be acquired by developing attributes such as dependability, determination, consistency, commitment, and compassion.

What does the long road have to do with God moments? The reality is, at times it might feel as if it's not a God moment at all. In today's society of immediate results and instant gratification, the long road may not look attractive. It may be something we prefer to avoid altogether. What's the point of taking a longer route when you can get there in a shorter time? But the long road produces the character and integrity we need for stability in life so our highs are not too high and the lows are not too low.

By this I mean that sometimes we have unrealistic and exaggerated expectations, such as thinking that because you've hit the happy jackpot of winning today, you will never suffer a loss again. Or assuming that because you've found the perfect spouse or have the perfect kids today, this euphoria will last forever. These blessings might create an emotional high for a season, but when the realities of life inevitably come, when the road feels overwhelmingly long, it will ultimately lead us to a devastating low because our expectations were unrealistic to begin with.

This is why balance is a beautiful thing. A sobering effect must happen in us to qualify us for the level of success God wants all of us to have. He never gives us good things to ruin us. He gives us good things to bless us, and it is the long road where we learn how to handle sustained success.

The long road may not be the path you are looking for, but it's usually the one you need. I thank God for the long road, for its beauty and lessons and unexpected stops along the way. Even for its bends and twists that I didn't see coming. This was especially evident as I walked alongside my dear sister Kay.

Waiting with Kay

Kay had battled cancer for several years and overall appeared to be winning the fight. I believed there was no reason the tables couldn't turn in her favor, giving her a once-and-for-all victory. She was a survivor. It surely wasn't her time to leave this world—at least not in my plan. However, when the doctor stunned us with the report that Kay only had six months to live, a new kind of waiting began that I'd never experienced before.

There were good days. Days that sparked hope in us that things would not be as the doctor predicted. We shopped, we laughed, we ate, planned trips, and did all the fun things sisters do. When the six-month time frame had come and gone without any real further decline, we celebrated. Maybe, just maybe, the doctor's report was wrong. However, as days turned to weeks, weeks turned to months, and months turned into years (two to be exact), things gradually began to change.

Watching my sister's slow decline was one of the most agonizing pictures I have ever seen. Watching our family take care of her was one of the most beautiful. I'd fly home for a few days, and then I was back on the plane again to be near her as much as I could. My daughter Lana was with me on so many of those trips. She was such a rock for our family at that time. There wasn't a project too big or too small for her. She just jumped in with both feet in the loving and encouraging way that only Lana can. Even with the loving care that was given to Kay by her husband, her children and grandchildren, my children and my precious sister, Elaine, we began to realize just how short our time with her really was.

No one could have told me the gift it was to care for Kay in those last months. It was truly my honor to love her, share with her, listen to her, to sing, laugh, and cry with her. To watch her say goodbye to everything she had lived for on this earth. Those were some of the richest, most painful, and yet most beautiful moments of my life. They were waiting moments. I am grateful for every last one of them. Grateful to have served her up to the final moments of her time here on this earth.

In those moments, not only was God teaching me, but Kay was teaching me as well. I'd become a student in the waiting moments. She was teaching me about resolve, about choosing joy in times of sorrow, and just how costly telling God yes could really be. Kay wasn't just dying; she was also grieving. She was grieving for those she was leaving behind.

I found myself spending more time with her than at home. And even when those responsibilities mounted, I knew I belonged by her side. My husband, children, grandchildren, church, and ministry all had to wait right along with me as I waited with her. I'm grateful for the grace everyone showed in those moments. To this day, members of my family and staff tell me things they learned through this process. Things that have helped them in their own long-road journeys. I heard countless stories of people in our church and those on social media who were making fresh commitments to their family because of what they witnessed in our walk with Kay. Others were grieving a loss themselves, and the fact that we were so public helped them not feel so alone.

Then the moment came, and Kay was gone. With that

moment, grief swept into the place where the waiting had been. While that wait was over, a new one began. The one between saying goodbye on this earth and looking forward to the day I will see her again. To continue on from such a moment, I needed all those long-road moments from the past when God walked hand in hand with me, assuring me that he would never leave me.

God's hope, peace, love, and strength have helped me find a certain measure of purpose in my pain. I could choose to be angry for the birthdays, anniversaries, Christmases, and all those special days that it appears the grave has robbed me of, but I choose to focus on the five-plus years I did have Kay beyond her original diagnosis. Seeing the purpose in the pain is all about perspective.

Times of waiting often forge in us things we can draw strength from for a lifetime. Walking with Kay through cancer was emotionally draining, stressful, exhausting, and heartbreaking, yet I will cherish the lessons I learned along the way forever.

> Times of waiting often forge in us things we can draw strength from for a lifetime.

The process of the long road should never be underestimated. It is vitally important to the journey. If we miss the process, we alienate ourselves from the promises God has made to us. As I write to you now, I can't say that I have all the answers about why things went the way they did, but I do know that the lessons I've learned on the long road have kept my mind and heart determined to let nothing separate me from the love of God in Christ Jesus.

Life happens and inevitably we will face disappointment, delays, and dead ends. Should you find yourself in such a place, confused about where you are in the process, here are a few things to consider.

A Work in Progress

If you've been to any major city, you'll inevitably notice a vast skyline full of mile-high buildings. We marvel at the design, layout, and expanse of skyscrapers but rarely think about what massive foundations must be laid to support the weight of what we see. A simple rule of thumb for skyscrapers is, the taller the building the deeper the foundation. Laying the foundation can seem, well, boring. Weeks and months of toiling on and below the ground with little to no view of ascension. But without it there would be nothing to build upon.

You may be waiting because your foundation is still being established. Don't try to build upward too soon; the foundation is worth the wait.

God Pours His Blessings into Structure

No matter where you live or what background you come from, I can almost guarantee something you and I have in common: we have a junk drawer! You know exactly where it is too. It's that place where you store life's little miscellaneous treasures that don't quite have a home.

Some are tiny little nooks—actual drawers—while some grow into full-blown episodes on the show *Hoarders*. However big yours is, it's a symbol of those things in life we'd rather deal with later. From time to time I find myself motivated to do something about mine. I pull everything out, throw away unneeded items, and place the rest back in as nicely and neatly as possible. And that works for a while, until more and more junk finds its way home.

I believe some of our waiting is because we haven't dealt with our "junk." It's that problem with our character that we file away in the corner of our mind to deal with later. But God longs for order in our lives. He wants us to deal with the things that are messy. He is a God who created the entire universe day by day, system by system, and molecule by molecule. Perhaps you are in a waiting season because God wants you to build some structure in your life.

"But where do I start?" you might ask. "I've got so many things in disorder." When life is overwhelming, I tend to start with the things I know I can easily conquer. Now, granted, these are just my convictions—and I encourage you to insert your own. But start where you can. You may not be able to completely transform your home Marie Kondo–style and "spark joy" as she so beautifully puts it, but you can do your best to attempt order. Clean up your car, make up your bed, and organize your closet. And while you are working on things externally, focus on what you are doing internally, like cleaning up your impure motives, dishonest tendencies, and judgmental attitudes. As you start making steps toward order, God will start giving you a strategy for the larger things that need structure, like your relationships, your finances, and your character.

And why does order do that? For me, as I start to conquer those small things, it declutters my plate, which minimizes my distractions. It's one less thing that demands my attention, positioning me to hear God more clearly. Life is loud, and order has a way of quieting the chaos. And it is in that quietness that I'm able to hear his still, small voice.

God Sovereignly Controls Our Life's Seasons

The wisest man who ever lived was named Solomon. Some of the wisest words he ever uttered are found in Ecclesiastes 3:1, where he said, "To every thing there is a season" (KJV). Understanding the sovereignty of God in seasons has been life-changing to me. We are not the author of these seasons, we don't own them, we didn't create them, and we have no say-so over *when* they happen, *where* they happen, or *how* long they happen. Only God has the power to change "times and seasons" (Dan. 2:21 KJV). If you don't believe that, go stand on the ski slopes in the Colorado mountains in December in your swimsuit and command the winter to cease immediately! I promise you it will not be long until you begin looking for the nearest fireplace. Save yourself and your reputation by accepting the reality that seasons are out of our control.

Most of us are not interested in challenging winter, spring, summer, and fall. We all know that making the wind blow, the sun shine, and the snow fall is above our pay grade. But when I began to realize this principle on a personal level, it brought me a measure of peace that settled so many issues in my life. I finally understood that once I did my part, the rest was up to God.

Hebrews 4:11 tells us that there is a "rest" that belongs to the people of God. One of the fastest ways to find his rest is by resisting every urge within you to attempt to control seasons that are out of your control. There is nothing that God has promised you and me that he will fail in fulfilling. The word he has spoken over our lives will never fall to the ground. He knows us name by name and face by face. As the songwriter says, "What God has for me *is* for me." What God has for you *is* for you, and he will make sure you get it in his time.

The Beauty in Waiting

Anything of real and true beauty takes time. The baby being born, the flower blooming, or the sculpture being crafted. You don't immediately see the beauty while it is in process. In fact, the finished work looks nothing like its misshapen or unformed beginning. But, if you take the time to watch the process, you just might see the amazing things that happen along the way.

Have you ever been to a series of sonograms of an unborn child? At the first appointment, all you can see is a little blip on the screen of a faint heartbeat, letting you know, yes, there is a living thing inside there. But on subsequent visits you see hands and feet being formed, the lengthening and curving of the spine, and the oh-so-important way to tell if it's a boy or a girl. Just like the baby, a flower takes its shape slowly with time as the green plant gives way to a beautiful blossom. And the dazzling art piece cannot be appreciated at the beginning, but as the artist shapes and forms it, molding it into its intended design, it slowly becomes a masterpiece everyone stands in awe of. So slow down; open your eyes to the things the busyness of life might be pushing you past. Sometimes real beauty is hidden in the smallest details.

Minka Disbrow waited seventy-seven years to see her daughter again. Once reunited, Minka discovered what God had done with her sacrifice and her years of prayers and waiting. Betty Jane, renamed Ruth, was adopted by a minister and his wife and had grown up in a loving family in Wisconsin. Ruth married a farmer and raised six children in a Christian home. Each of those six grandchildren has a story, including one who became a NASA astronaut and flew on four space shuttle missions and circled the earth 517 times. Ruth hadn't considered searching for her biological parents because her life was rich and full. Her son Brian brought the subject up, hoping for some help with his medical background but never expecting what they'd find. For all those years, Ruth's life felt blessed.

She had no idea she'd been prayed for, longed after, and cherished by a woman just seventeen years her senior.

But God knew.

When Minka turned 100 years of age, her granddaughter wrote a book about her experience titled *The Waiting*. The book released when Minka was a spry 102 years old. She still lived alone in Southern California, folded the programs for her church, attended Bible studies, and faithfully prayed—and now she had many more grandchildren and great-grandchildren to pray for. The family appeared on the *Today Show*, and the media picked up the story as it was shared around the world.

Minka grew up a poor dairy farmer in South Dakota, but her story was broadcast around the globe. Her interviewer was Jenna Bush Hager, the daughter and granddaughter of United States presidents. None of this was lost on Minka. When she peacefully passed away at age 102, Minka surely did so joyfully. God gave her the gift of seeing her prayers answered and all he'd been doing beneath the surface of that calm, unmoving lake.

Some of our most powerful moments emerge from the waiting moments. The steps we patiently endure really are taking us somewhere important, someplace we've been hoping to reach.

God is a moving God, and he will not leave you where you are. Waiting moments won't last forever. Don't stress over them, don't rush through them, and don't worry in them, because God makes all things beautiful in his time.

chapter four

Surprised by the Moment

A sense of helplessness swept over me that morning as I leaned close to the screen of my iPad to see my sweet newborn grandson on the video stream. Mason looked so tiny—too tiny in his incubator with tubes and wires coming out of his frail body. I watched his chest move up and down as he breathed, and I prayed his lungs would keep working, keep getting stronger. It was something we rarely pay attention to in ourselves and in those around us, the everyday miracle of our hearts relentlessly beating and the inhale and exhale of breath. But right then I noticed, because of the fragility in my grandson and the uncertainty of his situation, and all I could do was pray.

There are times in life when we are out of our league, when our hands can't fix something, when our words can't make anything happen, when our prayers are the only tool left in our toolbox. In those times, we find ourselves saying, "All we can do is pray." The words alone say, "I need help that is beyond me, and if you don't do this, God, it will not be done." All of us at one time or another have had, or will have, what I call the "end of me" moments. Moments when you realize you've done everything you know to do and so you humbly surrender your desires, aspirations, agendas, plans, pain, and perplexities back into the hands of God. Taking up that position can often leave us feeling frightened, vulnerable, empty, and defeated, but the truth is, once we realize "all we can do is pray," we find out prayer is the most powerful thing we can ever do.

When we pray, we are often at the end of us and we are looking to God and God alone.

On that morning, as I leaned in toward the image of Mason on the screen, I was about to receive a surprise gift from the Lord that would rejuvenate me and bring me enormous peace and joy. It was just a moment, but what a surprise gift it became.

When my twin grandbabies were born, Mariah was strong and healthy, but Mason had fluid in his lungs, along with a tiny hole in one of them, which caused him to lose weight in the days after he was born. With his breathing difficulties, he needed a breathing tube and remained in the neonatal intensive care unit (NICU) of the hospital instead of going home with his sister. His doctor said it would be a few weeks of struggle.

We all felt helpless. I wanted to hold that baby boy and just know everything was going to be all right. As a mom, it was overwhelming to know how afraid my daughter Nina felt. Yet I was so proud as I watched her and my son-in-law Travis's resilience and strength. The way our family came together blessed me. We are a very close family already. We work together in ministry, and our day-to-day lives revolve around supporting each other and sharing the ups and downs of this journey. We also have a close extended family, friends considered family, and church family. We have a wealth of great people in our lives. But when crisis comes to any family, it can either tear them apart or bring them closer together.

Once we realize "all we can do is pray," we find out prayer is the most powerful thing we can ever do.

When Mason and Mariah were born, it was a come-together time like nobody's business. We juggled the other grandkids, cared for little newborn Mariah so Nina and Travis could spend time with Mason in the hospital, and we all took turns at Mason's bedside making sure someone who loved him was always right there. Our church family around the world was praying with us, too, since we'd reached that point when praying was all we could do.

When I wasn't at the hospital, I was looking at that

video feed as much as possible. Whoever created the concept of streaming video inside incubators is a real hero to me. I was so grateful to be able to be home and there at the same time. It was comforting to log in and see him in real time. But what was comforting to me had to be uncomfortable to the nursing staff, as I found myself calling them constantly with my expert medical suggestions. "Can you pull the blanket down off his face? Can you tuck him in a little tighter? Can you loosen up the wire around his arm? He's been crying for three minutes and thirty seconds, can someone *please pick him up*? He needs his paci." I probably made fifty calls to that NICU. I can see them now, before they answered the phone: "Oh, great, it's Mason's grandmother again."

We were all exhausted and relying on God for our strength. My sister Kay's cancer was getting worse at this time too. So, on this particular day, in the midst of all that was going on, I really needed the Lord to give me an extra dose of him. I needed to know that he knew precisely where I was, what I was feeling, what I was up against, and the weight I was carrying. I had come to a breaking point. My faith was fluctuating, and I needed his help and his assurance. I needed to hear his voice speak louder than the doubt I had been hearing. I needed him to come to me, and he did! He came through a most unlikely, unexpected source.

First, please allow me to give you a little background about my mother. My mom was one amazing, strong lady.

She buried both sets of grandparents, both parents, two brothers, two husbands, and three of her five children. Her name was Rosie—Rosie Angel to be precise—which perfectly describes her nature. Mom was the type who was constantly working, cooking, cleaning, or doing something. We have an old VHS tape of her where she proudly exclaims, "One thing they won't be able to say about me when I'm gone is that Rosie was lazy." This was from a person who stood for eight hours a day working in a factory on an assembly line, often pulling double shifts. She would come home, sleep for a little bit, wake up and work in her garden, do chores around the house, cook dinner, cut her own grass, and wash her own car, because taking it to a car wash was truly a waste of money to her.

She was strong. And not just physically. My mother was strong in her spirit. What I remember the most about her was that prayer was a priority to her in her day. No matter how many hours she worked or tomatoes she picked or messes she cleaned up, going without prayer was *not* an option. Mom always knew that a prayerless life was a powerless life. When things got hard, she would always say, "I'm telling you, it's going to be all right. God's going to take care of us." And you know what? I believed her, because she was always right. God did take care of us.

Mom moved in with my husband and me when she was diagnosed with Alzheimer's disease around 2011. Quite a few years passed with only slow changes, some forgetfulness turning into more confusion. Then, in the last few years, Mom declined more quickly. Her moments of clarity shortened, except for once in a great while.

Mom tended to do the normal things someone in her condition does, like asking the same questions over and over. About thirty times every day, she would ask about her first great-grandson, Jaden. She wanted to know where he was, what he was doing, and when she would see him again. She would never fail to point out that Jaden was her favorite by saying, "That's my baby right there, and everybody knows it too." Now, don't misunderstand; she adored all the children, but there was something about Jaden. Many times when I would ask her about her other great-grandchildren, she would manage to maneuver the conversation back to him, asking, "When we gonna see him again?" I would always reply, "We'll see him at church on Sunday."

Momma always lived for God, and church on Sunday was a secondary consequence of her devotion to him. Even up to the Sunday before she went to heaven, she was *still* glad when we said to her, "Let's go to the house of the Lord." She may have forgotten the names of many people as she walked the road of this awful journey called Alzheimer's, but the one name she *never* forgot was the name of Jesus! Though, in her golden years, I never knew if her love for church was because of Jesus or Jaden. Either way, they both managed to put a smile on her face. As a matter of fact, we couldn't even get out of the parking lot after our service without her asking if we would be coming back next Sunday!

There's a slow loss that a family feels when a loved one has Alzheimer's. Mom was still there in body, but many things about her began changing. We'd all adjusted as much as we could, but, of course, I missed the personality of the mom I had known my entire life. The transition from being someone's child to becoming their caregiver can be more daunting than most could ever imagine, but if you look closely enough, you can see glimpses of beauty in it. As our roles began to reverse, affording me the opportunity to love, protect, and cherish her the way she had loved, protected, and cherished me, I gained a whole new appreciation for who she was to me. I knew the road wouldn't be easy. Walking people toward heaven in *slow steps* never is. Meeting her every need along the way would be my highest honor.

But there was one thing that hadn't changed: Mom still knew how to pray. I always kept a monitor in her room in case she needed me for anything. Because of that, almost daily, I could overhear the conversations she'd have with God. (Sorry, but not really sorry, for listening in, Mom.) To me, there's nothing more beautiful than the sound of a praying mother.

The birth of the twins was exhausting not only for my daughter Nina and her husband, Travis, but also for us, the family. It was amazing how these two little six-plus-pound human beings could turn an entire household upside down, but it happened. There were bottles to be cleaned, nipples to be sterilized, blankets, sleepers, bibs, burp cloths, and the tiniest T-shirts you have ever seen in your life to be washed. Not to mention the adults walking around with bags under their eyes, nearly numb from the lack of sleep that these new twin bundles of joy had brought into our world. And one of them had not even come home yet. It was pulling at my heart to know that my two little M&M's (Mason and Mariah), who had been coexisting in the same tiny space for nine months, were now separated and spending their days and nights far away from each other.

Then that morning came when Nina was at the hospital with Mason and I was at home watching the two of them via the live video feed coming from the NICU. I was leaning forward, watching little Mason on my iPad, when my mom came up beside me. She asked me what I was doing. I explained how Mason was facing a few health challenges that prevented him from leaving the hospital the day Mariah did. She was amazed that we could see him in his incubator, live and in the moment. Suddenly, it was as if Mom snapped back into her right mind, and she blurted out, "We need to pray for him." I remembered looking at her almost shocked, because I had not heard that much confidence in her voice in a long time. It was the same voice I had heard throughout the years whenever we were facing challenges. I was amazed at the clarity of her mind as she reached over, laying her hands on the iPad as if she were physically touching him. I knew in that moment that whatever she was binding on earth would be bound in heaven, and whatever she was loosing on earth would be loosed in heaven.

After she prayed for Mason, Mom looked me straight in the eye and said, "I'm telling you that baby is going to be all right. Mark my words. I'm telling you, Sheryl, he's going to be all right."

It is hard to put into words just how surprised I was in that moment! Standing there between four generations, I had without a doubt witnessed two miracles: Mason had just pulled something out of his great-grandmother and, in turn, his great-grandmother had just pulled something out of the heavens for him. Seeing him lie there, innocent and helpless to heal himself, provoked the protector that had been locked up in this prayer warrior, whose mind had been locked up by Alzheimer's. Never underestimate the power of a praying matriarch, for it was only a couple of days later that Mason was released from the NICU, and he and Mariah were reunited once again.

Not only was I surprised by this moment, but I felt as if it was a precious gift God had given me through a most unexpected source. He had used a very famil-iar voice from the *past*, to give me peace in the *present*, that *everything* in the *future* would be all right. It was a moment God gave me because I needed assurance that it was really going to be all right, and it was. That same peace came over me that I'd felt as a child when Mom would tell me God was going to take care of us. I rushed to the phone to tell the rest of the family. I kept telling them, "I have an amazing story that happened this morning with Mom!"

Some of the best moments catch us by surprise. They are God moments we didn't see coming. The Bible is filled with many instances where people were surprised by God moments. Mary and Joseph were certainly surprised to discover they were going to be the earthly parents of the Messiah. Like a lot of us, they had a much different plan, yet they were wise enough to be open to the divine interruptions of God. Proverbs 19:21 says, "Many are the plans in a person's heart, but it is the LORD's purpose that prevails."

Not only were Mary and Joseph surprised in the moment, but the shepherds who were out in the hills with their sheep were surprised as well. They were about to have a God encounter when they least expected it. As they were sleeping beneath the stars, the heavens erupted and an angel appeared to them, saying, "Glory to God in the highest, and on earth peace, good will toward men" (Luke 2:14 KJV). They were initially filled with fear, but the angel told them that the Savior, the Messiah, the Lord, had been born. These ordinary men had just experienced an extraordinary God moment! They

They had a much different plan, yet they were wise enough to be open to the divine interruptions of God.

didn't pause and question if they'd all lost their minds; instead, they grabbed their belongings and headed for town to see this newborn Messiah.

Then we have Saul, who later was called Paul. Initially he was a persecutor of those who were followers of Christ. Paul's complete transformation came one day while he was walking on the road toward the city of Damascus. A "light from heaven" flashed around him and was so great, he fell to the ground in fear. Paul was taken by surprise to be spoken to, blinded by, healed, and converted by the very God he had fought to discredit. It changed everything about Paul and his future. It transformed Saul the persecutor into Paul the disciple of Christ, who, by the way, became the writer of thirteen books of the New Testament.

The examples in the Bible are endless. Moses with a burning bush and a direct word from God; Sarah with a pregnancy when it seemed too late; the citizens of Jericho when the Israelites, walking around their city, suddenly shouted down their fortress walls; the parable with the father who, at long last, saw his prodigal son coming down the road. I could go on and on about God moments that have surprised men and women in Scripture as well as many of us today.

Sitting in a church service in Johannesburg, South Africa, recently, I heard the speaker sharing a true story about two grandmothers. Margaret and Ruth had both suffered strokes that left them partially paralyzed:

Margaret on her right side and Ruth on her left. Now, this kind of impairment is debilitating for anyone, but for someone who spent her life playing the piano, it was devastating. Have you ever suffered a sudden setback that made it seem as though life as you had known it was over? I'm sure Ruth felt that way as she sat at the piano in the rehab and recovery center. For Margaret, who was also in rehab, the feelings of helplessness were most likely mutual. But an ingenious therapist thought to introduce the two of them, and what took place as a result of this meeting was incredibly surprising.

As Ruth sat tinkering with her right hand, Margaret sat down beside her and began playing an accompaniment with her left hand. Chopin's "Minute Waltz" began to emerge from this duo's collaboration, and they discovered that life had not ended but had instead taken them in a surprising new direction.

It was the last thing anyone expected to happen. The two ladies were as different as they could be. While Margaret came to music more traditionally, Ruth says she learned by "osmosis" from her husband, who had written textbooks for piano teachers. But when you saw them perform, you would think they were born to do what they did, in exactly the way they did it.

Ruth and Margaret became so great at their new-found way to entertain people that they began receiving invitations to perform in senior-citizens centers, hospitals, and on television shows. Even the local newspaper ran a story about this dynamic duo. They appeared under the name Ebony and Ivory and wowed audiences with their seamless performances.

Both of these incredibly gifted women without a doubt wrestled with the apparent fact that music would never again play such a dominant role in their lives. How could it? The stroke each had suffered changed their lives forever. But much to their surprise, as well as the surprise of those who cherished them, what appeared to be a dead end ultimately launched them into a brand-new beginning!

It might surprise us as well if we knew just how many surprise moments God sends our way. Out of a place of weakness, my mother rose to the occasion, fighting through prayer for the life of the great-grandson she had never met. Two complete strangers, each in her own personal crisis, came together for the purpose of literally giving each other a hand so the song of their lives could continue to ring out loud and clear. I have come to the conclusion that God is full of surprises.

It might be a stunning sunset; a majestic, brilliant color-filled rainbow in the sky after a stormy day; a word of encouragement from the cashier at the store; a quote on social media that is exactly what we need to hear; a slobbery kiss from a baby; or a pet snuggling up at your feet with his unconditional love when your heart is aching. These are all moments brought to us by the God who loves to surprise us when we least expect it!

Here is how you know the surprise moment you are in has been orchestrated by God:

- God moments never contradict the Word of God. If a surprise moment goes against God's character or his Word, that's not from him, ever.
- They are a gift to you or the people around you. Remember, no matter how small or big, "every good and perfect gift is from above" (James 1:17).
- They may bring unconnected pieces together and suddenly offer clarity to a situation.
- They might correlate with other things God has done in your life. For me, hearing my mom say the exact words of assurance from my childhood, yet specifically say that our baby Mason was going to be okay, I knew that was God.

Remember, when given a gift, we should always say thank you. These are ways we can accept a God moment and show our gratitude for it:

- Be filled with the awe and wonder of that moment.
- Pause to really recognize it, and say aloud, "Thank you, God!"
- Respond to the moment. If God is telling you to do something, do it. Whatever the surprise is, there should be some kind of response.
- Acknowledge it by sharing what happened with

other people. Tell others what God is doing in your life, and they will be encouraged and have more faith in what God can do in theirs.

You see, God likes to surprise us. He gives us surprises every day, in little ways. Keep noticing, keep watching, and then the bigger ones will show up, like my mother's coming from a distant place to give me the sweetest assurance. What God has done for me, he'll do for you and more.

Mason had been in the NICU for two weeks before he came home. Mom's prayer gave every one of us the peace and strength we needed during that time. Her words will remain with me always as a special moment from God.

"Mark my words, Sheryl. I'm telling you, it's going to be all right."

chapter five

Managing the Moment

*If you've ever held a job in any capacity, whether at a fast-*food restaurant or corporate office, I think it's safe to say you know there are few things worse than having a bad manager. Unfortunately, at some point in our lives, we've all come across one. You know the type. Staunch dictators who take all the credit for your hard work, micromanage your every move, provide no clear direction, and show no visible signs of empathy or compassion. Some thrive on placing the blame on everyone else when things go wrong. Bad financial numbers are always the fault of someone else. When the numbers happen to be good, it's all because of his or her exemplary leadership skills. *Give me a break!*

In contrast, there are few things as motivating as having a great manager. Someone who actually leads, passing around credit and compliments like candy, asking for your input and actually listening, providing a clear path that you and your coworkers are to follow, and having enough emotional intelligence and empathy to hear you out when things get a little complicated at work. It is so refreshing.

Both types of people leave a lasting impression. As I described an example of a poor manager, your anxiety level probably started to increase as you gritted your teeth and threw imaginary darts at the picture of your last bad boss. The memories stir up so many emotions of anger and hurt because of how we were treated. Those people who have managed us well, we keep up with them on social media years after we stopped working with them. Maybe we cried at their retirement party. They meant something to us then and still do now!

So what is it that makes some people excel and others fail miserably? Certainly there are too many factors at play for us to discuss them all in this one book. However, I believe it has a lot to do with how well people have managed and mastered moments in their personal lives, how they've proven themselves in earlier, sometimes unseen moments and come out stronger, more mature on the other side. These were moments you and I were never privy to. Times when the pressure was on, they either blew it terribly or handled it with grace and tact. And even if they handled certain moments poorly, it makes a big difference if in hindsight they were able to look at them, learn, and grow from them. Even a bad moment has the potential to be a learning moment.

There is a driving force in all of us that wants to succeed. And no matter whether you are trying to succeed in your career or to be the best parent or spouse you can be, success will always require prior growth and preparation. The more we are driven to succeed, the more tolerant we become of the preparation process. Just like you take your time to look presentable and ready for whatever the occasion, God does the same with us. Before he puts us on display, he prepares us.

Does this mean God waits until perfection to use us? Absolutely not. The goal of preparation is not perfection but proving. Every leader, spiritual gifting, anointing, or business must be proved. What God uses, he first proves. This is the mark of any good developer, inventor, or entrepreneur. If the product you create doesn't work for you, how will it work for others? Before it can be used on a wider scale, it must be proved through practice, testing, and preparation. Without these tests, one will never know the potential of the product.

> Managing the moment we are currently in determines if we are ready for the next moment God has for us.

Leadership isn't for the faint of heart, and I have seen it chew up and spit out some of the best. How we handle the smallest and the greatest of our moments has long-term ramifications on the type of person we are becoming and will eventually be known as. Managing the moment we are currently in determines if we are ready for the next moment God has for us. There is no better example of this principle at work than the life of a young shepherd boy named David, who worked faithfully in his father's field.

The Field

Biblical days were days of planting, farming, seed time, and harvest. An agricultural society depended on the land. This is why the bulk of the Old Testament was about the owning and occupying of a territory. Wars were fought over land. It was left as an inheritance for generation after generation. Without land you had no place to build your house, plant your seeds, grow your crops, or raise your livestock to graze. Land was important.

But it was equally important to have someone work the land. In Genesis, God noticed there was no man to "till" the ground (Gen. 2:5 KJV). The word *till* means to manage, prepare, or make ready. When God placed Adam in the garden, this was Adam's moment to manage. The garden was Adam's field. Similarly, David was assigned the task of caring for his father's sheep and spent much of his time out in the field. There, he managed the flock, protecting them from predators, making sure they were fed and watered, and keeping them healthy so they could make their contribution to his father's household. In the stories of both Adam and David, their field experiences would prove pivotal to their purpose. For Adam, his care for the ground led to God's entrusting him with the care of Eve and the first family; and for David, his experience defending the sheep gave him the skills and confidence to defeat Goliath and step into a new stage of life. Their fields were places God used to grow, test, and prove them.

Whether we know it or not, we all will have certain seasons when we will be required to develop in certain fields. Don't underestimate the tiniest job you are doing. Just as the fields were pivotal to Adam's and David's purposes, they will be equally crucial to yours.

The field is a place of sweat and labor, full of moments to grow and prove us. It's not a place to be lazy. At the same time, the field can itself be a moment. It represents opportunity, service, and assignment. Just as our faith is given to us in measure, so is our field. It is our responsibility to care for and nurture that field, no matter how small it may start out.

Before God will trust you with a nation, he will test you in the field. Whether it is the garden of Eden or the field of David, every moment is molding and shaping us. The field is a place of preparation we are called to manage well. It's designed to test us the same way it tested both Adam and David.

The Field Tests Our Faithfulness

David was passionate about being a shepherd. He was faithful in taking care of his father's flock. God will always test your passion and faithfulness for someone else's field before he gives you your own. We see this principle played out throughout Scripture. Adam was faithful in God's garden. Joseph was found faithful in Potiphar's house. Faithfulness is an attribute we cannot neglect.

Have you been faithful to anyone else's vision other than your own? How important is it to you to work with someone else to make their dream a reality? God looks for faithful people first. How we manage the affairs of others builds character in us. The field is where he filters out our insecurities and inconsistencies so that we are proven faithful. The field is where true leaders are made.

The Field Tests Our Accountability

Now hang in here with me. I know you may not have wanted to dive into this section based on its heading. Accountability is not the hottest topic. Most of us, by nature, would prefer to answer only to ourselves. But managing your moments effectively requires accountability. David learned this in the field. His was by no means a luxurious job. Being a shepherd involved monotonous details like counting, feeding, watering, leading, and even defending the sheep. If one sheep left the sheepfold, not only did David need eyes to notice that it was missing, he also needed the ability to recover it. He couldn't slack off in his duties out of boredom or not wanting to do the harder aspects of the job; David was entrusted with the authority of his father to manage and protect the flock.

Whenever you are managing something valuable for someone else, there will always be the need for accountability. Accountability is defined as an obligation or willingness to accept responsibility or to account for one's actions. Every shepherd, at the end of the day, had to give an account of their dealings, including what was lost, what was gained, what was hurt, or what was destroyed during that day. Even though these were not David's sheep, he took personal responsibility for them as if they were. Being accountable is about owning whatever is under your watch.

Many times we mismanage moments because we lack accountability. Is there anyone in your life you are accountable to? Who have you granted permission to be honest with you about your choices, plans, and decisions? Is there anyone who can call you out, confront you, and correct your course when your choices are jeopardizing you and everyone around you? This may be hard to hear, but saying yes to correction is ultimate proof that you are committed to accountability. Being accountable and responsible in the small things is no "small thing" at all. It shows we have great integrity and character.

The Field Tests Our Endurance

Finally, the field is meant to test your gut, grit, and your drive. An old adage says, "If you cannot take the heat, get out of the kitchen." How do you handle it when things get hot? There isn't much shade in the field. In the field you are exposed to the elements. If it rains you will get wet. It is a place of dirt, heat, sweat, and labor. There weren't any neat people in the field. David smelled like sheep. David smelled like dung. David smelled like the field. It wasn't just something he did; it was part of his life.

I'm sure there were times he felt unnoticed and in-significant and wanted to walk away from it, but he didn't. Even while he was young, he must have been able to see the bigger picture, because I cannot find anywhere in Scripture where he complained even once about his assignment as a shepherd. Since God had chosen him to be a shepherd, being a shepherd was what David was deter-mined to do. He had settled that issue. He was okay with *where he was*, and it didn't matter who didn't understand that because David knew *who he was*.

How long can you feel insignificant before you quit? How long can you deal with being stuck in a stinky place? What is the shelf-life of your submission? The field is designed to test your endurance and help you answer these questions. David was completely devoted to his job. While it's not completely clear the level of David's fondness for his job, whether he loved being around stinky sheep all day or not, whether he complained or not, or whether he would rather be elsewhere or not, we do know he was committed to his post no matter what!

The Frustration

David had great potential, which we see realized later on in the Bible, but he submitted to playing his role as a shepherd boy, even though the conditions of his development were harsh and what many would consider to be unfair. He was the youngest of Jesse's eight sons and, in spite of his connection to his father, he was still reduced to the position of servant in his own house. He had to manage the frustration of being ostracized, overshadowed, disadvantaged, and devalued. He was stripped of the rights and privileges given freely to his brothers and was forced to spend his days and nights alone tending sheep. I will always believe it was David's lack of human relationships that caused him to place a premium on his relationship with God.

There were many moments in David's life when all he had was God. It was in those alone times with God that the real David started to emerge—the David who would eventually kill lions, slay giants, and rule nations. David the king was being incubated in David the shepherd. Why? Because greatness is often incubated in isolation. Without a doubt, David was called to greatness, but he was assigned to mundaneness. How do you handle being frustrated because your current situation looks nothing like your future potential?

These are the moments when the promises of God feel like sand slipping through your fingers. Moments when doubt is louder than hope. Moments that mock every prophetic word spoken over your life. If David was going to maximize this moment, he was going to have to manage the thing that made him miserable. Are you managing or succumbing to the things that make you miserable? David had to understand that, even in frustration, he still had a future. Although he couldn't see past the field, he still found favor with God.

> David was called to greatness, but he was assigned to mundaneness.

May I suggest this challenging period in David's life was "working for [him] a far more exceeding and eternal weight of glory" (2 Cor. 4:17 NKJV)? Don't be surprised if you find yourself encountering moments of frustration while reaching for the promises of God. It is how you handle these moments that determines your ability to advance beyond them. David's current moment was preparing him for future momentum!

And for someone who might be asking the question, "What's wrong with being a shepherd?" my answer is, "Absolutely nothing!" At the end of the day we all will be given the same "Well done, good and faithful servant," no matter how big or how small our task may be in the sight of other people (Matt. 25:21). There's nothing wrong with being a shepherd at all, unless you are called to be a king!

The Fight

What if the only thing standing between where you are and where God has called you to be is a fight? It might be the last thing you expected, especially on your journey with Christ. We're taught that "blessed are the peace-makers" and that we should "make every effort to live in peace" (Matt. 5:9; Heb. 12:14). Jesus himself said, "Peace I leave with you; my peace I give to you" (John 14:27). And though those scriptures are true, we are also encouraged to "put on the whole armor of God" and "fight the good fight of faith" (Eph. 6:11 KJV; 1 Tim. 6:12). You see, both ends of the spectrum are not mutually exclusive. As you strive for peace it doesn't negate that often significant moments are marked by a fight.

Jacob's name was changed to Israel only after a fight (Gen. 32:22–31). Saul's name was only changed to Paul after he was knocked to the ground (Acts 9). David was promoted from shepherd boy to king after his fight with Goliath.

It is interesting to note that David was used to fighting animals but had not been trained in tactics of warfare, especially to fight someone as colossal as Goliath. While his opponent had changed, his weapons had not. What David learned in his seemingly insignificant moments is what enabled him to defeat a significant giant. The same slingshot he had used in old battles, he used to bring down his new enemy. It's important to never get into today's conflict and disregard yesterday's weapons. If it was integrity, honesty, hard work, commitment, or sacrifice that got you there, let it be those same values that help keep you there!

It is also interesting to note that the giant David was fighting was immensely larger than anyone David had ever fought before. This suggests that standing between every significant moment is not only a fight but an opponent who is bigger than you. David had to be willing to deal with an oversized issue to transition from where he was to where he was going.

I'm not sure what your giant is. Chances are you feel that your opponent is bigger than you, your diagnosis is bigger than you, and the challenges you are facing are all bigger than you; but if you are going to be trusted with significant moments, you are going to have to be willing to slay significant giants. Don't be afraid. The field gave you everything you needed for the fight, and the victory is not in your size; it is in your swing. Make up your mind to fight. Believe in your weapon. Take your best shot. God has already gone before you, and the giants will fall.

Last, we see that David's fight went public. While most would like to keep our giants a secret, God often arranges a public fight to prove to you and everyone who is watching that *your last moment doesn't define your next move.* God wanted Israel to understand that, while the field was part of David's past, it would not be a part of his ultimate future. And how people perceived him to be was not at all who God had called him to be. Some battles require an audience, and some victories must be witnessed by others. God will not hide you forever. There will come a time when you will be faced with a fight that will usher you into your future.

The Favor

Needless to say, after David's epic victory over Goliath he quickly became a household name. Parades were held in his honor, and songs were written about his immense bravery. People even began comparing him to the current king of Israel, Saul. His public fight proved he had favor with God, but these public celebrations proved he had gained favor with man.

Note the favor did not come to David because he asked for it. There was no vote, drawing, or poll that could have possibly named him as the winner. He wasn't next in line for the throne, nor did he have training in military warfare. David found favor because he mastered the ability to manage a hard moment. We have all had to work our way through hard moments. Whether it was rejection by someone close to us, the death of a family member, the loss of a job, a divorce, or a bad diagnosis, it's our ability to manage the difficulty of those moments that reveals the destiny of the next. Favor is a real force.

It is a head-on collision between conflict and calling. Whenever conflict collides with calling, it produces the undeniable favor of God!

In addition to David's ability to manage hard moments, he understood that if he was going to maintain favor, he was going to have to remain focused. While slaying Goliath and being anointed as Israel's next king was more than enough to give him notoriety, David returned to his father's house and continued to tend sheep. David didn't allow favor to cause him to neglect his current assignment. If we are going to be the leader that God has called us to be, we must never allow "what's next" to distract us from "what's now." David understood that his ability to remain faithful to this moment would qualify him for many moments to come.

Never allow ambition to cause you to neglect where you are in the pursuit of where you want to be. Take a moment and evaluate any unfinished business you may still be carrying from your past. Did you finish the work of the last season, or did you leave it undone in a rush to get to this one? How did you leave the last church you served or your last place of employment? Did you finish your assignment (what you had been tasked to do), or will someone else have to pick up the slack of a work you left unfinished? Make no mistake about it, leaving past assignments the right way can be daunting, but the integrity of a person is not determined by their favor, but rather by the condition in which they left their field.

The Finale

Matthew 22:14 tells us, "Many are called, but few are chosen" (KJV). The fact that you are reading this book signifies that you have heard the call! Don't devalue yourself and despise where you are; refuse to underestimate where you are destined to go. Even if you are struggling with feelings of inadequacy, God will use moments to make us into what he has called us to be.

Moments are a gift. Don't miss them! Don't be intimidated, overwhelmed, or frightened by them either. Every moment measures and prepares us. Every moment has value. Every moment matters. How we manage our moments, both large and small, determines what doors God will open on our behalf. If we are faithful even in just a few of them, God will make us ruler over many (Matt. 25:21).

chapter six

Faith in the Moment

People who look at my life today could probably never imagine that I've had days I wanted to quit. Days I've wanted to throw in the towel. Days when I didn't know if life was worth living. But I have! I know what it's like to be in over my head in trouble, in depression, in defeat, and in debt. If the Enemy would have had his way, I wouldn't be alive to tell you my story. If he had prevailed, I would never have been a wife, mother, pastor, or preacher, let alone an author.

In my earlier days, never-ending challenges gripped my courage like a stronghold, blinding me to everything God had already written into his plan for my life. As hard as I tried, I couldn't see myself becoming any of the things I am today. The role he had scripted for me to play was only made possible when he took what was hanging *over* my head, placed it *underneath* my feet, and used it as a platform on which he would position me for the performance of my lifetime. And he orchestrated it all using an unseen force called *faith*!

Unseen faith is exercised daily by billions of people around the world, believers and unbelievers alike. For instance, when you woke up this morning you had faith that your smartphone (or alarm clock if you're old-school) kept the right time and that the alarm would go off at the precise moment you needed it to. You laid your head on your pillow and closed your eyes the night before, fully placing your trust in a small device filled with microchips, glass, and wires to ensure you woke up in enough time to get to your job or start your kids on their way to school. Then you either made yourself breakfast or stopped by a restaurant to eat, without a second thought as to how safe the food really was. Some of us then got into cars, fully believing that our mode of transportation would get us from point A to point B malfunction-free.

Air travel takes an even greater level of faith. If you've flown multiple times, think about the progression of your faith from the first time you took to the friendly skies until now. I can remember how nervous I was on my first few flights. I prayed the night before, on the way to the airport, as I was boarding the plane, as it was taking off, while it was in the air, while we were landing, and then finally one last "Thank you, Jesus" as I exited safely from the aircraft. My faith was extra, deliberate, and more aggressive because the experience was so new. A lot of us aren't wired to embrace new things easily. They can raise our level of stress and cause us to lean more on our faith simply because of a heightened sensitivity to new environments. Let's face it: climbing into a large steel tube with little room to move around and leaving the earth's gravitational pull at breakneck speeds isn't exactly the most relaxing experience in the world.

While we're on the subject of flying, it really takes faith just getting to the plane. Faith that you'll get through the early morning traffic. Faith that the security lines will be manageable. Faith that your bags will be transferred to the proper place so that when you arrive in Dallas your bags don't arrive in Cleveland. Faith that you'll make it to the right gate. Faith that you board the right plane. Faith that the air traffic controllers are in sync with the technology they have at their disposal and that the thousands of planes flying that day are being routed to the right destination without incident. Now that I think of it, the bicycle seems like a wonderful mode of transportation. It takes *faith to fly*!

So what is faith? What is this invisible but oh-so-tangible attribute we depend on so desperately, even when we're not aware we're using it? If that sounds like a complicated question, it is! How do you approach the amazing, all-knowing, all-encompassing Creator of the universe with simple childlike faith? Let's see what the Bible has to say about it.

The book of Hebrews describes it like this: "Now faith is the assurance (title deed, confirmation) of things hoped for (divinely guaranteed), and the evidence of things not seen" (Heb. 11:1 AMP). It's like the wind. You may not see it, but when it blows you will feel it. You can't always trace it. You may never know where it's coming from or going to, but you do know it's real. In my analogy of the plane, it is knowing that even though I cannot see gravity, I have confidence that because of the force of the engines working, together with the shape of the plane and the wings, gravity will not prevail. While I may not see most of the pieces at play working to ensure the plane takes off, by faith I believe in them and eventually see the evidence of that belief.

The apostle Paul said in the book of Romans that each of us has been given "a measure of faith" (12:3 KJV). The word *measure* doesn't sound so grand. In fact, in the original Greek translation the word is *metron*, which means a "limited portion." This might be appalling to you to think that a God who is totally unlimited would place a limit on our portion of faith. And though it might be appalling, it should not be surprising, because the principle of stewardship has always mattered to God. He makes it very clear in Matthew 25:23 that if we are faithful over a few things, he will make us ruler over many. So the good news is that whatever your measure is, you have the power to grow it.

Even as you are reading this, you need to know that your capacity for faith can be increased. The faith that qualified Abraham, Jacob, Joseph, Sarah, and many others to take their place in the Hall of Faith (Heb. 11) was *faith* that had multiplied and matured. It empowered them to believe the unbelievable, see the unseeable, and know the unknowable. There is nothing God commended more than faith. And when our faith honors God, in return God honors our faith.

Faith in the life of the believer is critical, because the way God ultimately communicates with us is through our faith. For example, faith is to us spiritually what finances are to us physically. They are two different types of currency, but both are meant to be used as an avenue of exchange.

If you want a pair of new shoes, you exchange money for them. In the same manner, when I give God my faith, he in exchange gives me what I am in need of. That is why the Enemy is after our faith. He understands its value. He understands our faith is what gives us the authority to operate in both earthly and heavenly dimensions.

Whatever you do, fight the good fight and hold on to your faith. And please believe me when I say there are moments when your faith will require a fierce fight. I remember back in 2002, when my husband had a major surgery. We were both incredibly anxious about the decision to go forward with the doctor-recommended procedure, but we knew it had to be done. After much research, thinking, and dialoguing with each other and with God, we scheduled the date and arrived at the hospital early in the morning.

I stayed by his side as long as I could, trying to help him relax and know that everything would be all right. Nothing I said, did, or prayed seemed to be working, but when the anesthesiologist came in . . . *everything* changed! Whatever it was they put in his IV immediately took the edge off. I gently kissed him goodbye, and as they rolled him down the hall, I wanted to say, "Hey, wait, could I get a little bit of that stuff you gave him?" I didn't, though. Something told me God probably wouldn't be pleased. Besides, it was my job to watch and pray. What should have taken four hours ended up taking nearly eight. Those extra hours of waiting and praying, which turned into pacing and praying, began to feel like an eternity. What in the world could be taking so long?

Historically, surgeries didn't happen for my husband without some type of hiccup. After one previous surgery, the doctor came out of the operating room and into the waiting area, running his hands through his hair. He said, "Whew, we lost him," followed by a *long* pause. When he realized I was speechless and one millisecond away from falling face forward into the floor, he finished his sentence, saying, "Oh, but we got him back, though. Oh yeah, no worries. We got him back!" I can't even begin to describe the myriad of emotions I was feeling as I stood there looking at that doctor. I wasn't sure if I wanted to hug him or punch him, but the one thing I *was* sure of was that God was good, death had been denied, and it would not have the final word over my husband's life!

Fortunately, the bedside manner of the surgeon we were working with now was much different. When he did emerge from the operating room, he assured me that though it had taken longer than they had planned (after being 80 percent complete they had to abort their original plan and implement a new one), all had gone well and my husband was resting comfortably in the ICU. I was relieved.

After a couple of hours, I was allowed to see him. He appeared to be resting well, but the doctor was somewhat concerned about his lack of kidney function. You see, unlike most people, my husband was born with only one kidney. The fact that it wasn't functioning was a bit concerning; however, they were not quite ready to label it as an all-out emergency. Actually, they informed me that if I needed to go home and get a few hours of sleep that this was a good time to do that. I knew sleep was out of the question, but since my daughter was there with him, I decided to run home, shower, and change clothes.

By the time I arrived at home, it was a little after 4:00 a.m. I walked into the house as quietly as I could, in an attempt not to wake up my mother, my two other daughters, my sister and brother-in-law, and my father and mother-in-law as well, who were visiting with us at the time. I hadn't been there for ten minutes when my phone rang. The moment it did, I had a feeling it wasn't going to be good. When I answered it, on the other end of the line was my daughter Lana. I could tell through the fear that had gripped her voice that something had happened.

"Mom, they need Dad's kidney to work *right now*! If it doesn't they are going to have to do some kind of procedure on him. Dad's really upset! We need you to get back here to the hospital right now!"

I told her I would be right there and hung up. To say I was scared is an understatement. I was literally shaking. The sound of her voice, the pressure of being on high alert the entire day, the lack of sleep and food—it all took an immediate toll on me. In the blink of an eye, my imagination had gone wild, and my faith felt as though it had all but vanished like a vapor into thin air. I ran to my closet and, as I began to put on my clothes, something came over me. Out of nowhere I found myself becoming angry. But this was not just anger, this was more like rage! The best way I can describe it is found in Genesis 3:15, where God said, "I will put enmity (open hostility) between you and the woman, and between your seed [offspring] and her seed; He shall [fatally] bruise your head, and you shall only bruise His heel" (AMP). The audacity of the Enemy to think he was going to attack my husband's life *again* and I would simply sit on the sidelines paralyzed with fear. Absolutely not! Not today, not tomorrow, not now, not ever!

I stepped out of my closet, yelled upstairs, and told all my family to wake up, because I needed them to meet me in the living room. I yelled downstairs for my sister and brother-in-law, asking them to join me as well. I knew it was time to come together as a family and draw a line in the sand. If we had to fight, then let the fight begin! And, standing in the middle of my living room in Raleigh, North Carolina, in the wee hours of the morning, we joined hands and declared war! We cried out to our God, asking him for a miracle, and we reminded our Enemy that, as we came together in the name of Jesus, he would have no other choice but to back up! FYI . . . there is something powerful about a family that prays together! The kind of prayer that comes from a united family is a weapon, and when it is launched, it can deconstruct any and every plot the Enemy has formed against us.

We prayed the prayer of faith in that moment together. Then I got in my car, drove back to the hospital, and walked toward my husband's room. The closer I got, the more I could hear commotion. I opened the door, and, much to my surprise, he was surrounded by hospital staff and lying in a bed that had been completely inverted.

"What is going on?" I asked.

They began telling me about some kind of last-ditch effort they were doing to get his kidney working. I will never forget the horrified look on his face as they brought his bed back into its proper position. He was not happy, and neither was I. Obviously, the hospital staff wasn't happy either, because despite all they had done, the little bag that holds the urine was still completely empty.

Since all we could do was wait, and because other patients needed attention, one by one the staff walked away, leaving me, him, Lana, and our God with the room all to ourselves. As things began to quiet down, he did too. I had no idea what the doctor was planning next. All I knew to do was to fill the atmosphere with prayer and praise as we waited on the Lord. Sitting there next to his bed, my faith was in a fight, and I knew this was a fight I had to win. I needed *faith* in that moment! There was no room for doubt in this moment. I knew that if this kidney would ever function again, it would be because of God. So I held on. I reminded myself of his faithfulness in my life. I reminded myself that we had just come together as a family, touching and agreeing. I reminded myself that just because things were too much for me, that didn't mean they were too much for *him*.

I didn't know how or when this would turn in our favor, but I refused to give up. I didn't have the option of giving up. My faith in God was all I had. And sometimes you don't know how important your faith is until it's all you've got, but if you'll dare to believe, it will become everything you need it to be! I can tell you this today with a bold assurance because, while sitting there in the fiercest fight my faith had ever been in, I looked up and noticed the little bag that had been completely empty was now well on its way to filling up. While I was fighting it out, God was working it out! And when the doctor walked into the room, I pointed to the bag, and out of his own mouth he said, "*That* is a *miracle*!" He said the very words I had believed to hear, because God had done the very thing we had believed he would do!

Faith Reinforcers

We have heard it said that faith is like a muscle. Muscles are meant to be flexed. The more you use them, the stronger they become. The problem with many of us, however, is we keep waiting for a faith we can feel. But that's not how faith works. Stop waiting for what you don't have; use what you do have when the moment comes, and watch God increase your measure of faith.

Here are a few steps I personally believe you can use daily to grow, enlarge, and reinforce the capacity of your faith.

Cultivate Perspective

Whatever you feed will grow. One Sunday afternoon, on a flight back to Dallas, my mind was consumed with some issues I had been dealing with. The more I thought about them, the bigger they seemed to get. Eventually the issues consumed my entire train of thought, and before I knew it, I found myself feeling hopeless.

My focus on the situation forced out any possibility of a solution. My perspective was off. Deciding to make a mental shift, I focused my attention out the window. As we were approaching Dallas, I noticed how small things looked. From buildings to cars to houses and even highways, it appeared as if I could grab the entire city in my hand. How in the world could I have ever gotten lost in something so small? But let's face it: whether it's a city, a circumstance, or a situation, being *in it* feels so much different than being above it. The reality was, the buildings were tall and the city was enormous, but when I was on top of it, it all felt manageable. Faith doesn't make things easy, but when you merge it with the proper perspective, it does make them possible.

> Faith doesn't make things easy, but when you merge it with the proper perspective, it does make them possible.

My view of Dallas that day showed me that I had allowed the small things that were concerning to me to become bigger than they really were.

Whatever you are facing today that is challenging your faith, keep it in proper perspective. And, instead of bracing yourself for failure, why not stretch your faith and embrace the possibility that you might just succeed? How are you cultivating a proper perspective?

Cultivate Confidence

Another key faith reinforcer is having a working knowledge of your identity in Christ. If I asked you the question, "When God looks at you, who does he see?" what would your response be? It's highly probable that

God's view of you and your *belief* about God's view of you may be completely different. Looking at ourselves, we tend to see our faults and failures, our mishaps and mistakes. But when God looks at us, he sees our potential. He sees us through the *finished work* of the cross. He sees us through the lens of his eternal plan for our lives.

You do know that your life was planned, don't you? It doesn't matter how you got here, or whom God used to get you here; you are here because of his plan. He told Jeremiah, "Before I formed you in the womb I knew you, before you were born I set you apart; I appointed you as a prophet to the nations" (Jer. 1:5). "'I know the plans I have for you,' declares the LORD, 'plans to prosper you, and not to harm you, plans to give you hope and a future'" (Jer. 29:11). God is telling us here that before we ever took our first breath, smiled our first smile, made our exit out of the womb and our entrance into the world, the plans for our life had already been laid. He's telling us we have been marked, branded, and chosen, and that his signature on our life has set us apart.

You are different, and he meant it to be that way. You are unique, unmatched, and uncommon, and he meant it to be that way. You are *not* a mistake. You are *not* an accident. You are the handiwork of God. Whether your parents loved you or not . . . God did! Whether they had plans for you or not . . . God did! Whether they wanted you or not doesn't really matter, because . . . God did!

And knowing this is imperative because there's no way you can know how badly he wanted you and not walk with confidence into what he has called you to!

You can possess an unbelievable boldness on the basis of your relationship with the One who called you. When my grandkids come to my house, they don't question what's available to them. Because of the history they share with me and their papa, they know exactly who they are to us. They know exactly where they stand with us. When they arrive, they either run upstairs to play or run to the refrigerator to eat. Understanding who they are gives them confidence about what they have access to. I can take them to my next-door neighbor's house, and, even though it's close to mine, the experience changes drastically.

Knowing who they are and what's available to them makes all the difference. The same applies to our faith. Knowing how God sees us, what he's planned for us, what he's given us access to, and what he has emboldened us to possess steadily reinforces our faith.

That's why it's imperative that we invest the time to know how God sees us. To look for what he's planned for us, not just the grand finale that will erupt in applause and bring the house down, but each little stage that enlarges incrementally over time. Think about how many Broadway performers today had small beginnings that first took place in church plays and community centers. Even before that, they were performing in living rooms and on fireplace ledges to audiences made up of only family members who would clap and cheer even if they were bad! Every stage along the way helped cultivate the necessary confidence and steadily reinforced their faith for the future. What can you do to further cultivate your confidence so you can walk in faith in each pivotal moment on your path?

Cultivate Community

Unless you live alone in an underground bunker in some undisclosed location for the rest of your life, being around people is unavoidable. In fact, we were designed by God for connection and relationships with others. Genesis 2:18 tells us, "It is not good for the man to be alone." Surrounding ourselves with the right kind of people is so vital to us as we strive to build our faith.

As you may have guessed already, I'm a big proponent of family. It's the single most important part of my life. I am so incredibly blessed to be part of a strong family unit. I don't think a day goes by when you couldn't find one of us encouraging another. I realize someone reading this book might say, "My reality is so different from yours, Sheryl," and I'm very aware that may be true for many of you. But God is even more aware of that, and he tells us in his Word that he "sets the solitary in families" (Ps. 68:6 NKJV). That means you can trust him with the community he places you in. Whether it's a community you were born into or one he chooses to set you into, God will make sure the environment he places you in will be conducive to the growth of your faith.

Along with the family community that God so graciously gives us, we should also invest in those we know we can count on to speak truth into our situations. Their honesty may be hard to swallow today, but it might just spare us from unnecessary pain tomorrow. The right people aren't blind to the realities in your life, but they choose to believe *with you* that things will get better. They will encourage you as you are preparing to interview for that new job. When your children are making wrong decisions, they remind you of all the things you invested in them over the years. They help paint a picture in your mind of possibilities even when you can't see them for yourself. They are *for* you. They are *with* you. They are bridge builders and gap fillers. When you are weak, they are strong. They love you when you're right and when you're wrong. They are your tribe, and, because of that, no matter what you may face or what you may find yourself in, you are never in it by yourself!

I've found that God will speak through the community of people you've come to love and trust, whether it's a word of encouragement at just the right time or a hope-filled text that tomorrow will be better than today. And should the shoe ever shift to the other foot, you will instinctively become to them everything they have been to you, because that *is* community—and when it is cultivated correctly, that *is* what community does! What steps are you taking to cultivate your community so you can be bridge builders and gap fillers for each other in those harder moments in life?

Cultivate Perception

If perspective gives us oversight, perception gives us insight. Perception is a way of regarding, understanding, or interpreting something. Many times the battle of our faith is won or lost based on our perception. When things happen that are unplanned, unwanted, or unwarranted, we may start to view things inaccurately. An inaccurate perception can have you running away from things you should be running toward, avoiding things you should be confronting, and can be preventing you from reaching for things God has already given you permission to have. A healthy perception, however, chooses to see things through the lens of faith. It magnifies opportunity over opposition. In 1 Samuel, David's brothers saw Goliath as the opposition, but David perceived him as an opportunity. Anyone who discovers treasure will tell you it is often found wrapped up in trouble.

Countless numbers of people have made their greatest advances in life while standing face-to-face with adversity. They refused to lie down in hard times and chose to search desperately for opportunity rather than subject themselves to defeat. Sir James Dyson, whose wildly popular Dyson vacuum cleaners are a household name, tried 5,127 prototypes before getting an acceptable working model. Had his "give up" threshold been like the average person's, he could have easily quit. Can you imagine trying something more than five thousand times? His perception enabled him to look at five thousand mistakes and see them as five thousand opportunities.

The reality is that people often fail more than they succeed, but a properly cultivated perception of faith, in that moment, makes all the difference. We can either cry over the doors that have been closed, or we can celebrate over the ones that have been opened. Always remember, it's the closed doors that make the open ones more obvious. How are you cultivating a proper perception so when the moments of opportunity come you can see them clearly?

Faith Reducers

If God uses things to reinforce our faith, then there must be things the Enemy uses to reduce it. One of the faith reducers everyone has experienced at one time or another is the spirit of comparison. President Theodore Roosevelt once said, "Comparison is the thief of joy." In my estimation, nothing kills gratitude quicker than comparison. That is reason enough to make conquering comparison a goal in our lives.

God has made each of us uniquely and individually. The Bible says we are "fearfully and wonderfully made" (Ps. 139:14). The Creator of the entire universe looks at us in wonder and amazement. He formed us with his very own hands, and yet he designed us to be singularly fascinating to him. So, knowing this, why do we diminish how he's made us by comparing ourselves with others, particularly when his Word clearly says this is unwise? (2 Cor. 10:12). Anytime we look to other people as our reference point, we will always find ourselves coming up short.

> Anytime we look to other people as our reference point, we will always find ourselves coming up short.

And yet we tend to do this in so many areas of life. Our car is not as new as our neighbor's, or our house isn't as clean as our younger, prettier sister-in-law's house. Our career isn't as glamorous, or our vacations aren't as expensive. Comparison causes us to look at our future with despair rather than hope, because we feel we will *never* get to the position in life that everyone else is in. Why do we do that to ourselves? Why do we continue to gauge our success on the basis of the accomplishments of others?

Social media has not helped us in our comparison obsession either. If anything, it has accentuated our fears and insecurities to ensure we're "keeping up with the Joneses." Social media giants like Instagram and Snapchat develop filters so we can artificially improve our overall look for the public. Even the people we follow aren't really telling us the complete story. They are taking a snapshot of their best day and convincing us it's their everyday, and it makes us believe that our ordinary day is inconsequential compared to theirs. Buying into that for any length of time will dismantle your faith. The Bible tells us that if we really want to get ahead in life, godliness with contentment is the route we want to take, because "godliness with contentment is great gain" (1 Tim. 6:6).

We must realize that we have been designed to find our value by having faith in God, cultivating our faith in such a way that recognizes God has us on his perfect path no matter where we *feel* we should be. Hebrews 12:2 admonishes us to run the path of our lives, "looking unto Jesus the author and finisher of faith" (KJV). Looking at anyone else leaves me looking into an inaccurate mirror. When we "look unto Jesus," he becomes the mirror that gives us an accurate picture of who God intended us to be, freeing us to see with a clearer perspective as we approach the moments of our lives.

Comparison is toxic! It will rob you of your focus, your faith, your time, your self-worth, and ultimately your true identity because it takes you from being an otherwise grateful person and gives you a thousand reasons you shouldn't be who you are. Don't let it take root in your heart and chip away at your faith in the moments you need it most.

Not only does comparison reduce your faith, but so do disappointment, doubt, fear, and unbelief. All these things come to break down our faith, because it is our faith that gives us peace with God. Our faith is the substance we exchange for those things we are hoping for. We are justified by faith (Rom. 3:28). We are established by faith (Acts 16:5). We are sanctified by faith (Acts 26:18). We are purified in our hearts by faith, and it is through faith that we obtain the promises of God. Wow! If I were the Devil, I'd be after your faith too.

Without a doubt, there are times when the subject of faith can seem so complicated; but as I bring this chapter to a close, I want to encourage you to never lose sight of its simplicity. Hebrews 11:6 says, "Without faith it impossible to please him: for he that cometh to God must believe that he is . . ." (KJV). If you really want to please him, it's as simple as just believing him. Believe he is who he says he is. Believe he will do what he says he will do. People do all kinds of things trying to please God, and many ultimately end up exhausted from all their human efforts—efforts that will not count nearly as much as simply taking him at his word.

God says, "If you really want to please me, I need you to *believe me*. When I tell you that you are the head and not the tail, above only and not beneath, *believe me*. When I tell you that you are blessed in the city and in the field, *believe me*. When I tell you that your latter house will be greater than the former, *believe me*. When I tell you I have called you, anointed you, and I've brought you to the kingdom for such a time as this, *believe me*. Because when I tell you I am going to do something in your life, nothing will please me more than knowing you choose in that moment, by *faith*, to *believe me*."

chapter seven

Honoring the Moment

My hope is that, at this point in our journey through this book, you've started to discover as I have that our lives are actually a collection of moments. From significant life-changing highs, such as a birth of a child or getting married; to debilitating lows, such as experiencing a death; to those small, unexpected, seemingly insignificant moments that in hindsight were much bigger than they appeared—all moments matter.

Some moments easily stay ingrained in our memories because of how they affected us. We're able to say, "It was on this specific day, at this specific time, that I experienced this, and it led me to the following." Others are more like brief time periods that somehow led you to become a different person. No matter how we experience them, they all matter. And that is why it's so important to realize that to make sure we don't miss the moment, we must take time to honor every moment and season we are in. This means, rather than constantly trying to skip past them or failing to see how God is using them, choosing to see their significance and being thankful for his work and the people he's working through in each moment.

> To make sure we don't miss the moment, we must take time to honor every moment and season we are in.

If I've had a measure of success in my life, whether in my career or personal and family life, one thing I know I can attribute it to, outside of the sheer grace of God, is that I try my best to give God thanks in all things. Notice that I didn't say *for* all things but *in* all things. My family and I joke about an acronym I use all the time in our group texts when anyone mentions or celebrates an accomplishment in their lives. It's TGBTG, and I'm sure you can guess it stands for "To God Be the Glory." I know you've probably heard that term mentioned loosely in church before as a cliché from people who don't really mean it.

"You sang so great today."

"Who, me? Oh, to God be the glory."

That phrase can sometimes have a feeling of false humility. But there really are a lot of people who are genuine in realizing that all glory goes to God for any of their accomplishments. That's how I try to live my life as well. On my own, I realize I am incapable of accomplishing much of anything. Any time I see the hand of God moving in my life, I'm quick to recognize that it is him. It's one of the ways I keep my soul anchored and my absolute focus on God, knowing that anything he's called me to do is only because there is a greater plan that is ultimately for his glory.

One of the ways I honor God for the many seasons he's allowed me to experience is to honor the people who have been strategically placed in those seasons, especially acknowledging the foundation of a godly heritage. Never underestimate the power of pouring a firm foundation for your family. This sets you and future generations up to take hold fully of every moment God sets in your path.

To this very day, it is the *yes* of my father and my grandfather I'm still standing on. It was the decision they each made years before I was born that ultimately set the stage for my life. Before I drew my first breath, took my first glance, let out my first cry, smiled my first smile, and took my first step, it was their obedience that cleared the path and pointed me in the direction of my life's purpose. Decisions like my grandfather saying yes to the call to preach would ultimately lead my father to do the same. Their acts of obedience led me to accept that same call several years later.

By the grace of God, I have traveled all over the world. I've been blessed to minister in places they may have only dreamed of. And even though they may have never physically traveled outside the United States while they were here on earth, they have gone every step of the way with me. Every person who has decided to follow Christ, every family that has been restored, and every person who has been given hope through anything God has ever done through me can all be traced back to them. I am an extension of all those who have gone before me. No matter where God takes me, I know I did not get there by myself. Their *yes* created a ripple effect that I believe will continue on through my children, their children, and generations yet unborn.

Of my nine grandchildren, there is a good possibility that many of them may not stand behind a traditional pulpit as I do. Their pulpit may never be a Bible stand, but as they decide to serve the Lord and walk in kingdom principles in their lives, families, and career paths, they are doing the work of ministry! For that reason alone, every moment I spend with them I am intentionally strengthening their foundation of faith.

My mother is another one of those godly influencers in my life. I can't tell you how many times I've stood ministering to people and, as I spoke, thought to myself, *Wow, I'm sounding so much like my mom. I wonder if people even realize that while they are listening to me they are actually hearing her?* That should come as no surprise, as she has been the loudest and most consistent voice in my life. Whether it was a ride in the car, sitting at the kitchen table, or even things she would say in passing, her words built belief systems I still live by to this very day.

I often emphasize the importance of having "clean hands and a pure heart" (Ps. 24:4). I know those words originated in the Bible, but I heard them first through my mom. She would also say, "Be sure your sins will always find you out," which to this day helps me remember that there's no hiding anything from God. He sees it all and knows it all. I also often think about times when our family was in a tight place, when she would instinctively at the right moment say, "God is going to see us through this . . . I guar-an-tee you he will!" And one of the greatest lessons she taught me was how to be a giver. She modeled the importance of being faithful to God in her finances.

One of the moments I will never forget is when she was lying in a hospital bed, nearing the latter part of her life. I remember her looking up at me and asking, "Sheryl, who's paying my tithe?" With so many things to be concerned about in that moment, including her health, children, and well-being, with needles and tubes in her body, she still had the mind to say, "Who's paying my tithe?" It's because God was an absolute priority to her, and her entire life was a message to me.

Like my father and grandfather, she may have never dreamed of getting up in front of people and ministering to them the way I have been blessed to do. Her congregation was her family, and let me tell you, she pastored us well. There was never a time in my life when I don't remember my mother giving honor to the Lord and teaching her children to do the same. From her example of excellence in everyday chores, to praying with us through good and bad times, her life was an open book to honor God.

I began to honor the moments with her more and

more as I realized God was speaking to me through her wisdom and insight. Our influences might have been in different arenas, but it was her wisdom and life experiences—moments, if you will—that gave me the courage to embrace mine. And so I learned to lean in when my mother spoke. As a child I *had* to listen to her, but as an adult I *got* to listen to her. And no matter how long I live, I will always honor her—along with my father and grandparents—for the firm foundation I have been blessed to build on.

What I Decide Today Determines What I Experience Tomorrow

It's no secret my grandchildren are everything to me. Having them has changed my life for the better in so many ways. It's made me more aware that the decisions I make today ultimately have an impact on what they will experience in the future. Isn't that true for all of us? Decisions are far-reaching. They never just affect us. Which is why our decisions must always be wrapped in prayer. In fact, there are things you will pray for that you may never see with your own eyes. But pray for them anyway! Just because what you pray for doesn't happen in your generation doesn't mean it won't happen in your house.

When my mother was able to personally see the blessing that my children live in, she was actually witnessing her mother's prayers being answered. The dress my grandmother prayed for is hanging in my closet. The church my father prayed to build, I am building. The book my grandfather prayed to write, you are holding in your hand right now. They never stopped hoping, they never stopped praying, they never stopped believing. Because of their diligence I'm walking in a generational blessing that I believe will continue for generations to come.

Every Step Matters

Another way we can honor the seasons or moments we are in is to realize, as the Bible says, that unless the Lord builds the house, they labor in vain that build it (Ps. 127:1). No one starts to build a home until after an architect has put the right plans together. In any building project, sequence matters. If you attempt to build the roof without first pouring the foundation, I doubt you'd be in the home-building business for long. So, in the same manner, understanding that God orders our steps makes a big difference in how we perceive things.

Think of it this way. Have you ever been in a holding pattern on an airplane? A holding pattern happens when weather conditions between the runway and the airspace you are in are not conducive to landing. An experienced pilot knows that within a few more minutes the weather will clear, allowing the plane to land with no impediments.

There's nothing wrong with the plane or the runway; it's just that the atmospheric conditions between where you are and where you need to be are unstable at best and unsafe at worst. The plane will begin circling until the time is right, and the decision is made solely for the safety of the passengers. Sometimes holding patterns in life are part of God's plan. We don't expect them, we don't include them in our travel time, they frustrate us, but eventually we arrive safely because someone other *than us* had their eye *on us* and helped us get to our intended destination.

When we start viewing our lives through the lens of the Master Architect, we will stop allowing ambition to drive us to premature decisions. Ambition is a strong desire to achieve success. Sounds fairly harmless at first glance. But ambition has a way of slowly progressing into a disruptive force that can derail us from God's plan and cause us to miss the moments that matter the most. Unbridled ambition can cause us to push down doors that God himself wanted to open. It can cause us to live in a constant state of fear that we are missing out on our destiny because we haven't achieved it in the time frame we set for ourselves.

Notice I didn't say in the time frame God set for us, but in the time frame *we* set for ourselves. Unchecked ambition will cause you to trample over everything in your way trying to get to the top. As if destiny is a one-stop shop or a single location! It will cause you to discount, step on, or step over the very people, relationships, and experiences God intended you to encounter to assist you along your journey. I cannot emphasize enough how every single step, even those that seem inconvenient and unnecessary, really does matter!

Learning to submit in holding-pattern seasons can leave us vulnerable and feeling as if we have no control. However, it is our willingness to honor God by submitting to his time frame that will guarantee we arrive at his intended destination for our lives without incident. When you've done all you can to stand, just stand. Peace prevails, and mental conflict ceases the moment we realize and remember that controlling outcomes will always be above our pay grade. That's a job for God and God alone!

You Define Your Success, Not Others

A young man shared a story with me a few years back that I've never forgotten. He and I didn't know each other at the time, but he attended a service I was ministering at in Greensboro, North Carolina. According to him, he was at a crossroads in his life where he felt he should be further along than he was. He's a very driven person, and he felt the ambition of wanting "what's next" was starting to get the best of him. His plans for where he thought he should be, how much money he should make, his marital status, and how far he was on the path toward purchasing a home had all missed their deadlines. Nothing seemed to be lining up. Then he said something that made me chuckle. It would be nice if every person I've had the opportunity to minister to retained what I've said, revisited their notes, and rehearsed over and over what they heard. But, in reality, sometimes it's a different story. This was the case with this young man. He explained, in all honesty, he couldn't remember anything I'd said that night, except for one statement. One statement! That's it?! You mean to tell me you missed the profoundness of my introduction? The depth of my knowledge of scriptures? *And*, my mesmerizing oratorical abilities? SMH. Yep, the only thing he recalled was one solitary statement. Man, God has a way of keeping you humble. What he remembered was, "Success is simply being able to look back over your life and see how you've progressed from one year to the next."

Now that I read that back to myself, it *was* a pretty good statement. Sorry—what I meant to say was, to God be the glory! But let's reflect on that for a minute. Success is simply being able to see signs of growth in an area. For this young man, hearing those words that night freed him from his self-imposed mental prison. He no longer had to meet the benchmarks he created for where he thought he should be. He was now free from living in the comparison trap. He simply had to start moving the needle forward in every area of his life to improve it and begin defining his own success.

If he could look back and say, "I used to be selfish in this area, but I can see that I'm not anymore," or "I used to have a hard time forgiving, but I'm a little better at letting go now," that would be true success. By allowing

God to help him improve and grow, day after day, week after week, month after month, and year after year, he began progressing. When he tells that story now, he concludes that over time most of the things he truly wanted in life God gave to him, and much more. The difference is, it was all done according to God's ultimate plan for his life.

His perception shifted drastically when he honored where God had him at that particular time, even if he hadn't progressed at the pace he had planned. I'm so glad our encounter in Greensboro had such an impact on this young man named Marc Jeffrey. Shortly after our meeting, he met and eventually married my daughter, Lana, becoming my first son-in-law.

I can almost hear some of you saying to yourselves, "Well, you don't know what kind of year I've been having. I went backward in some areas in my life. Actually, things got worse rather than better." And you know what? You might be right about that. But did those difficult times teach you anything? What did you discover about yourself that needs to change? Were there hidden weaknesses you didn't know you had? Why is that important, you might ask? Because if you can't identify areas of weakness, you'll never know when you start to improve on them.

Even if it feels like you are losing ground, it might just be God pulling you back in order to propel you forward. Failure under the right perspective is such a gift. When you're in the middle of failure, it feels like, well . . . you've failed. But if you've never experienced the beautiful gift of learning from your failure, please trust me on this—if you can learn from it, you can grow from it. I remember standing at an altar many years ago, feeling defeated by some of my life's choices. As I stood there with a heavy heart, the pastor walked up to me and said, "You can make a mistake and not be a mistake." Those words, to this day, are life-changing to me. They not only changed the trajectory of my life then, but today I often use them to help others who feel the same way. It's possible to miss the mark but still reach the goal.

Sometimes the fact is we do fail, and we all have people in our lives who are quick to point that out. People who are negative, judgmental, and self-righteous. But when you encounter those people, just know they are a distraction from the bigger picture

> Even if it feels like you are losing ground, it might just be God pulling you back in order to propel you forward.

God is trying to show you. Stay away from those people at all costs. Love them from a distance . . . and leave them there! Instead, look for people who will motivate you, push you, and challenge you to be a better you.

God will use voices like a mentor, pastor, or even this author to help you realize he wants to do more in your life. Honoring the moment means being the absolute best you can be with the tools you have at your disposal right now. You may be clueless in regard to your career, but you can be diligent and resourceful at your current job. You may not have the highest pay scale that you want at the moment, but you can learn to be frugal and save what you do have. God will always bless your attempt at order and structure. That's just his way! So, whether you can track how you've improved on a map or you simply became more aware of areas you need to grow in, you've experienced success.

The Badge of Honor

In closing this chapter, I want to share with you a few things I've learned along the way to help you honor every moment you are in. Adopting this as "your way," I believe, will keep you from missing some of the most valuable moments God wants you to encounter. Those who are going to wear the badge of honor must know the importance of these principles.

Treasuring Your Troubles

I *love* to bake. Well, the truth is, I love baked goods, and I try my hand at baking. Especially at Christmastime. My daughters have picked up the same love for it over the years. It's just become one of our holiday traditions. An important step to baking a great cake is knowing how to mix the right ingredients together. The more from scratch the cake is made, the more precise the ingredients need to be. None of them by themselves are very tasty. As a matter of fact, if you started to eat separate ingredients alone, they could be downright distasteful. Try eating a stick of butter by itself, then follow it up with a full cup of flour, and wash it down with a glass of vanilla extract. You get the point! It's the blending process that makes what was once disgusting become delicious. Life is no different.

Some things we find ourselves trying to swallow can choke out our very existence. These are the hard places of life. Burying a child, which is something we were never wired to do, is a hard place. Walking a parent through debilitating diseases like Alzheimer's is a hard place. Reversing the role of parent and child as you daily watch them pack up a part of themselves you will never see again is a hard place. Losing a job, home, car, or relationship are all hard places. Hard places redefine our lives and our self-esteem and leave us simply . . . tired.

Have you ever just been tired? Slept all night but woke up tired? Tired of reaching, tired of the grind, tired of the hustle, tired of taking two steps forward and three steps back, tired of seeing the lack of progress, tired of trying. Perhaps, like Jacob in the Old Testament in Genesis 28, you have found yourself so tired that you've taken a rock and used it for a pillow. It's not the pillow you are accustomed to. It's not the kind of bed you prefer. It's not even the environment you are used to lying down in, but when you're tired, like Jacob, you learn to make the best out of a bad situation. He rearranged the rocks, laid his head down in a hard place, and God appeared to him there.

Life is full of hard places. I'll never forget the day I

had to teach this lesson to my daughter Tina. She was eight at the time and had just been chosen to be a part of the local softball all-star team. When she arrived home from school, to her surprise, she noticed a For Sale sign in the front yard of the rental home we were living in. I remember her asking me, "Mom, why is that sign in our front yard? Does it mean we are moving? And if we move, does that mean that I can't be a part of the team?"

This was certainly a hard place for me. We *were* moving, and I was going to have to find a way to help her see that life will throw you curveballs when you least expect it, even if you are on the all-star team. As I broke the news to her, tears began to pour down her face. She was so proud to be a part of the team, and now, out of nowhere and because of no fault of her own, she was being uprooted.

She ran upstairs, wrapped herself up, and lay down in her bed. I gave her some time before following and sitting down beside her. I began walking her through what it meant to make sacrifices. I talked to her about how often life requires us to lay down, to let go of, or to walk away from things we love. "So," I said to her, "this is probably not the first and it most definitely will not be the last disappointment that you face in life. But you have two choices: (1) you can view it as a disappointment and become bitter, or (2) you can view it as a sacrifice and through it become better."

I was trying to help her have proper perspective. I told her that God knew her heart and would always bless her when she made the right choices. Then, in the most profound way, she looked at me and said, "Instead of all these little sacrifices that God keeps asking us for, can't we just once and for all simply give him our life?" I couldn't have said it better myself. Somehow, I think her eight-year-old mind was trying to find a way to process the painful places that would inevitably be a part of her future, and the way she decided to do that was by just settling the fact: "I'm just going to give him my life." That night she wrote her first song. I still remember the lyrics to this day:

It's just a simple sacrifice
a simple sacrifice
a simple sacrifice of . . . giving your life.

So, as you find yourself in a hard place, feeling forced to eat life one ingredient at a time, always know that, though hard places are never comfortable, they are priceless. For without them we would never find him, because God lives in hard places, and he will meet you there.

Celebrating Your Beginnings

I've often heard people use the scripture in Zechariah 4:10 referring to not despising the day of small beginnings. These words are a great reminder to us when we are in the beginning stages of building anything. Whether it is a marriage or a family, a business or a career, starting can often be difficult. Zechariah 4 is that "chicken soup for the soul" type of scripture that helps us recognize that beginning stages, even though they may be small, are not necessarily bad. Surprisingly, people tend to overlook the second half and most important part of that verse, which reads, "For the LORD rejoices to see the work begin" (NLT). Just reading that makes me happy.

You probably never thought you were the one who could make God smile. But when he sees your courage to just begin something, that's exactly what he does. Whether it's a New Year's resolution, a weight-loss goal, starting to organize your closet (Lord, help me!), becoming more conscious of your mental health, or starting the process of forgiving someone who did you wrong, there is power in starting the process. There's a promise in making a fresh start that says you won't stay stuck where you are. For if we are consistent in our commitment and don't give up in our efforts to move forward, we set ourselves up for a better end. "Better is the end of a thing than the beginning thereof" (Eccl. 7:8 KJV). God's just awesome like that. He gets happy when you start and makes sure that when all is said and done, we're better off than when we started. I'll take that deal *all day.*

Remembering Relational Honor

The ultimate picture of relational honor can be found by looking at the cross of Calvary and specifically the relationship between Jesus, the Son of God, and Mary, his devoted mother. In light of everything he was experiencing at the worst moment in his life, he anticipated the things she would need long after his death and asked his mother to take care of his best friend and his friend to take care of his mother. Though he was carrying the weight of the sins of the world on the cross as the Son of God, he still never forgot he was also the son of Mary. It seems unbelievable that he would be able to think about someone else so intentionally when he was only moments away from death. But he made certain she would never be alone when he was gone. Seriously . . . *who* thinks like this? And *how* do you think like this, seeing that the presence of pain makes most of us self-centered?

How did he find the strength to anticipate what she would need tomorrow, while he was still in the middle of so much personal pain today? I believe it was because he was very aware of the relationships that were strategic in his journey. People like Mary, who fed him, held him, cradled him, consoled him, dressed him, and even taught him his first words. People like John, who was there from the earliest parts of his ministry. John didn't only know *about* Jesus, he also knew him personally. He walked with him, served with him, witnessed miracles, and when it would have been easier to abandon Jesus, like so many others did, John stood faithful at the foot of the cross. Looking down, Jesus saw them both. Looking forward, he saw they would need each other. This significant act teaches us how much relationships matter. They mattered to Jesus. They should matter to us too.

For many of us, like Jesus, it was our parents who

helped us get to where we are today. The Bible clearly draws a line of significance when it comes to honoring our parents. In Exodus 20, honoring your father and your mother is not a suggestion; it's a commandment. Notice that it doesn't say honor what they have done toward you, but it says honor them because of who they are. They were chosen by God. So whether they were good parents, bad parents, or indifferent parents, whether they gave you the thing you felt you needed in life or they didn't, we still honor them because God used them. Quite frankly, if he hadn't used them, you wouldn't even exist. Perhaps they may not have had the best parenting skills or a great financial legacy to leave you. Maybe there were many things you needed to know that they were incapable of communicating. Maybe they were absent altogether. But God wasn't. He was there, and he made you a part of his plan. You can rest assured that when you don't get what you need from those you thought you would get it from, God *still* has a way of making sure you get it!

Maybe, for some of you, he used a mentor, a coach, a neighbor, a pastor, or a friend to help point you in the direction of destiny. Whoever they may be, their entrance into your life was a God connection. No matter how far you go or how high you may rise, remember the importance of pausing to recognize and celebrate those who have paved the way for you to be where you are. And here's a little secret: honor is not only something you need to give, it is also something that those who have helped you need to receive. Relational honor is reciprocal. Thank those who have affirmed you. Thank those who have talked you through tough times, dark nights, and foggy places. Thank them for the emotional missing pieces they brought to your life and for seeing things in you that you didn't see for yourself. As you honor others, God will honor you.

Large and Small

I want you to know with all my heart that your legacy, what you are remembered for, is hardly revealed "in the moment." It's a collection of both large and small, significant and insignificant moments that make up the whole. What you are doing today, right now, even by reading this book, is a moment that will make a lasting impact.

If you shared your faith with someone this week, you honored the moment God presented you. If you made the choice to treat someone with love and kindness who treated you harshly, you honored the moment. If you paused today and said, "God, I don't understand where I am in my life, but I thank you that you are working all things together for my good and your glory," you honored the moment. My prayer is that your spirit is on high alert for the moments God is sending your way. I pray that you will start to see more and more of them for what they are: God moments! And as you encounter them, honor them and help others recognize God moments in their lives too!

chapter eight

Missing the Moments

It's the crack of dawn in Dallas, Texas. The house is silent, and the scent of steaming coffee in my mug further perks me up. I breathe. I inhale the goodness of God, while exhaling with gratitude. These moments at the start of my day are precious. They are clear and undeniable moments spent with the life-changing God. There is no way in the world I can experience them and be the same.

But not every morning begins like this. Not every morning begins in the comfort of my own home, in my own space, unmoved by the fast pace of life's demands. Not every day goes as planned. Some days are derailed with one distraction after another. We oversleep, waking up in full panic mode, because lunches still need to be packed, clothes need ironing, kids need to be fed, calls have to be answered, e-mails need forwarding, and, without fail, somewhere between the front door and the car door there is always a neighbor with a question, a concern, or a request. Whatever they need just becomes one more thing to add to the morning to-do list! I sometimes wonder if the helping-the-neighbor thing can count as points with God, seeing as he emphasized it so strongly in his Word—the Word, by the way, that I likely didn't have time to look into! That same Word that is a lamp unto my feet and a light unto my path.

Well, I guess that explains it. No wonder I have days when I feel as though I can't see my hand in front of my face, let alone know where to put my foot next! I've gotten caught up in my own busyness and missed those critical start-of-the-day moments with God that set me on the right path. I'll be honest: most of the time, when I find myself struggling to navigate the weeds of my life, it's my own fault! Somewhere I've come up short in the "sold out, committed to Jesus forever and for always" area of my life, and it affects all the other areas too. Unfortunately, I don't always realize what's going on at the time. I wonder why I'm struggling, why it feels like God has hung a Do Not Disturb sign on heaven's door! It is one thing when I don't talk to him; it is a completely different thing when he doesn't talk to me. I take that personally! To be honest, sometimes the silence of God can be shocking, leaving me wondering if the two of us are on speaking terms at all. There have been days when I've even shaken my head in dismay, wondering what he is up to and why he may or may not have allowed certain things to occur in my life.

Someone reading these words right now might be wondering how in the world I could say such things. Well, this may come as a shock to you, but I'm not the first person to feel like this, and neither will I be the last. As a matter of fact, even the *greats* in the Bible struggled with these very human feelings. Take John the Baptist, a forerunner of Jesus. Even he went through a similar season when he began questioning God.

For a while, John's popularity was unrivaled. People were mesmerized by him. People loved him. Like a magnet, they were attracted to him. What was the attraction? It couldn't have been his attire or his physical appearance that drew people to him. John, you see, was a bit rough around the edges. He dressed daily in camel's hair and ate wild locusts. Who eats locusts? Eating locusts wasn't even cool in biblical times, but what *was* cool was the way people felt when John spoke. Something happened inside of them. Something came alive. The proverbial light would come on, causing many to follow him loyally and listen intently to what he would say.

But, over time, things changed. John, their leader, the man who led them into repentance, baptized them, and radically brought new meaning to their lives, was arrested. The one who had brought clarity to their purpose was now sitting in a prison cell, confused himself. How do I know he was confused? Because he'd just pointed Jesus out in the crowd, saying, "Thou art the Christ" and now he was asking the question, "Art thou the Christ, or do I look for another?" (Matt. 11:3, paraphrased).

How could the pendulum of his faith swing so drastically? How could the man who once had the power to draw people from the city into the wilderness to listen to him preach the same message over and over again now be questioning the most important truth he'd ever known? Well, let's start with saying, life happened. Life happened, and John was thrust into the middle of a tumultuous transition.

Transitions can happen in the blink of an eye. Not only to people like John the Baptist, but to people like you and me, single mothers, single fathers, entrepreneurs, philanthropists, and CEOs of Fortune 500 companies. From baby boomers to millennials, from Gen Xers to Gen Zs, transitions happen to us all. Just like *that*, the right set of circumstances could come together and produce the perfect storm. We have all been there, blindsided by out-of-nowhere distractions. It can leave us stunned and disoriented, wondering what just happened? How did I get in this? More importantly, how do I get out of this? I don't have time to be sidelined.

You know that feeling when you're driving down a highway toward an important destination, when time is of the essence, and you suddenly realize, *I just missed my exit!* Of course, the highway is packed with land-mines of drivers on the verge of road rage, and the next exit is nowhere in sight. *How will I get back? Where can I get off?* The clock on the dashboard seems to be flashing, "Not only are you late, you're about to miss it altogether!" And your GPS is shouting, "Recalculating!" then insisting that you "make a U-turn!" Like compound interest, one problem leads to the next and on to the next. It happens to all of us, and the effect can be stressful, to say the least.

Life's detours and delays are annoying and can leave us frustrated. And it is difficult to be frustrated and focused at the same time. Sometimes the detours are of our own making, and sometimes, as in John's case, life just happens. But God's voice, like a GPS, will talk us through the delays and unfamiliar terrain until we are once again safely pointed in the right direction. Turning a missed moment into a God moment is possible if we will listen for his voice. The hard part is that his voice doesn't always come in ways we expect. Sometimes it's blatant and booming, and other times quiet and calm.

> Turning a missed moment into a God moment is possible if we will listen for his voice.

This is important to realize, because most of the time we aren't looking for a quiet God to point the way. A subtle message isn't what we naturally expect. He's the Creator of the universe who spoke everything into existence. I imagine God's voice like an infinite roar, shouting, "Let there be light!" God's voice ordered molecules and atoms to coalesce and form matter. His voice created the planets and set them upon their orbits. As we stand beneath the night sky with the starry diamonds sparkling against the pitch-black universe, it's because of the magnificent God who created all that we see and even more than we can imagine. His words knit together the genes and cells of a man from the dust of the earth. None of that sounds like a quiet God to me.

And so we sometimes miss what he's saying. We miss the opportunities to turn a detour into a God moment, because we expect those moments to reveal themselves in grand fashion. We picture those ta-da moments: the great job promotion, the marriage proposal, the surprise opportunity, and the life-changing encounter. While these are amazing milestones in our lives, there are thousands of other important moments that are more subtle in comparison to the blatant, obvious, and loud.

God's Quiet Voice

God often speaks to us in whispers like the "still small voice" we read about in 1 Kings 19:11–13 (KJV). Many times he unveils his plans, preparations, and purposes through the most unassuming people and in the most unassuming ways. Many years ago, I was preparing for a ministry opportunity at a large event I was looking forward to. I felt this was going to be a God moment in my life. But I was about to discover that it was not how I had envisioned it at all.

At the last minute, literally as I was walking toward the pulpit to minister, I was informed there had been a change of plans. I quickly returned to my seat. To say I was stunned at the seemingly spur-of-the-moment decision would be an understatement. Not only was I stunned, I was confused as well. On top of that, my feelings were hurt. I truly felt like my God moment had been pulled out from under me. How could that be? If it was really a God moment and it was really mine, how could someone make one decision and make it all disappear like a vapor?

I stayed for the remainder of the service, then returned to my hotel later that night. I would like to say how resilient I was in that moment, how I blew off the whole experience and bounced back like nothing had happened. But, in reality, that wasn't the case at all. The struggle was real. It was more real than I care to admit.

I was young in ministry and not as confident in my calling as I would later become. A moment like I had just experienced had the potential to knock me off course before I even had the opportunity to get in the race. Through prayer, I had to wrestle down the thoughts I was feeling, while pleading with God to "create in me a clean heart and renew a right spirit in me" (Ps. 51:10 KJV). I could live without this ministry moment that I felt was stolen right out of my hands. I could also live without the person who stole it as well. What I couldn't live without was having a clear line of communication between God and me. And for that to happen, I knew I had to let it go.

It wasn't fair, but I had to let it go. It wasn't right, but I had to let it go. And while standing there ironing a shirt to wear the next day, with tears rolling down my face, I made an intentional decision to do just that . . . *let it go*! I had tasted bitterness before, and it was not something I wanted to be a part of my everyday diet. I may have missed the opportunity, but I was determined not to miss the moment. Nothing I had experienced that day was worth my missing out on all the things I *knew* God had planned for me. And because of that one conscious decision to quiet my heart and trust him with the outcome, God leaned in my direction. As I stood at that ironing board, he said something to me I still remember to this very day. One sentence that totally reframed my thinking: "Sheryl, I'm the man in your life, and I will get every door for you!"

Suddenly it all started to make sense. My disappointment was not a dead end. What I thought I missed wasn't the end of the story. From that day on, something shifted in my mind. I began to see God more and more as "the man in my life," and a true gentleman at that. I can honestly say, from then until now, I watched him open more doors than I have even been able to walk through. When he says he will pour you out a blessing you will not have room to receive, he means it.

The truth is, a God moment can't be stolen. What I thought was a missed moment was really a moment of insight. What God has for you is for you. It might not turn out the way we think it will, but trust me when I tell you he is in every second of every moment of every hour of every day working everything together for your good.

Things That Distract Us

Innumerable things can keep us from seeing, hearing, and experiencing the subtle God moments that come our way. The good news is, once we start identifying what diverts our attention from God moments, we will cease being distracted.

Here are just a few that can potentially slip under the radar of our lives redirecting us away from our destinies.

Overly Busy Lives

Let's face it: being busy is a choice. We may claim we are too busy, but usually we make things that are important to us a priority. Busy lives distract us from hearing the voice of God.

Entitlement and Pride

It's never a joyful experience when we examine our own lives and see the not-so-beautiful parts. Our sinful nature can sneak into our lives through an attitude of entitlement, pride, or arrogance. If it's always about us, our needs and our wants, it's possible that we may be more self-centered than Christ-centered. And that needs to change. Just remember that attitudes like these will keep us at a distance from God. First Peter 5:5 tells us that "God opposes the arrogant but favors the humble."

Distrust and Lack of Faith

There are many times when it feels like God is keeping us in the dark about his plans, leading us by bread crumbs down an unfamiliar path. In times like these, it takes a solid faith to keep us moving through the darkness when the light of day can't be found. Without a solid foundation in God, when the going gets rough, we'll find ourselves looking for the nearest exit. But trusting him completely, we can settle into his plans for us even when we can't clearly define what they look like. That assurance comes from knowing that he who began a good work in us will be faithful to complete it. (Phil. 1:6 KJV).

Fear

Fear can be crippling. It can creep in like an invisible mist, debilitating us, severely restricting our movement, and blinding us to our own resources. A rabbit has the ability to escape a lion's attack, but because the sound of the lion's thundering roar is so ferocious, the rabbit finds itself paralyzed and unable to flee. It forgets it can run into small places that the lion could never get into. As a result, the rabbit becomes prey to something it had the power to get away from all along.

I learned a long time ago that we can never allow fear to have the final word in our lives. Talk back to fear. Remind yourself that "God hath not given us the spirit of fear, but of power, and of love, and of a sound mind" (2 Tim. 1:7 KJV). The only power fear has over you is the power you give it. Begin being fearless today!

Missed Moments Will Happen

Missing subtle God moments isn't something new, so let me give you hope. Even people in the Bible missed moments, while others seized them. In Romans 15:4, we read, "For everything that was written in the past was written to teach us, so that through the endurance taught in the Scriptures and the encouragement they provide we might have hope."

Let's look at a few people and be encouraged to grasp our moments.

Ruth and Orpah

In my estimation, one of the most beautiful pieces of literature that has ever been written graces the pages of the Old Testament, and it is called the book of Ruth. In it we find the story of both Ruth and Orpah. They were sisters-in-law, newly widowed, and had come to a point where they had no idea what their futures would hold. The road ahead was unknown and certainly filled with challenges.

After the death of her husband and sons, their mother-in-law, Naomi, informed them that she had decided to return to her homeland. Upon hearing of her decision, Orpah's and Ruth's responses couldn't have been more dissimilar. Ruth was adamant that Naomi could not leave her behind. Orpah was equally as adamant that no matter what the two of them did, she wasn't ready to go anywhere. Both of these young widows had the opportunity to change the trajectory of their lives. Both could have embraced a new beginning, seized a new moment, and seen a much more hopeful outcome, but Orpah found the changes she would be required to make to be too challenging. So, while standing on the edge of a new horizon, Orpah kissed her mother-in-law goodbye, and that would be the last we would hear of her. She would die just as she lived in a place called Moab.

Ruth, however, heard something Orpah didn't hear, felt something Orpah didn't feel, and knew something Orpah didn't know. Out of her lineage would come the Messiah, the Deliverer of the world. Therefore, getting out of Moab would not be optional for Ruth. She would make the move and she would make it because it wasn't just about her, but it was about what would eventually come through her. Jesus was locked up inside of a woman, who was locked up inside of Moab. She found the courage to break free from what Orpah would die in. Two women, two stories, two moments . . . Orpah would miss it, and Ruth would seize it.

The Innkeeper

It is nearly impossible to talk about Joseph, Mary, and the birth of Jesus and not talk about the innkeeper. You know, the one who failed to make room for the Messiah and his mom, leaving her to bring him into the world in such a dark, cold, lowly place as a manger. Throughout history, he could've been known as the man who made room for Jesus—the man who made room for the deliverer of all mankind to be delivered. Imagine living life knowing you were a part of making such a profound moment happen as opposed to missing it.

He didn't realize the opportunity that was presented to him.

He had no idea that this story would be told for generations and generations to come. Unfortunately, he would be known for the rest of his life, and beyond, as the innkeeper who embarrassingly missed the most significant moment of his life.

Sure, it was a busy time in the city of Bethlehem. People were coming in droves to be accounted for in the national census, and here arrived this young man with a very pregnant wife in obvious need of help but without a reservation. The clueless inkeeper had no idea that the Savior of the world was at his doorstep. Remember, moments are often subtle and easily missed. We have to seize them when they present themselves.

There's nothing that says his future was adversely affected by turning away Mary, Joseph, and the soon-to-arrive Jesus. Oh, but what a monumental moment to have missed! Missing out on being there, on offering help, and living the rest of your life knowing you were part of this moment. Out of all the moments that came his way, this was most assuredly *not* the one to miss.

The Priest and the Levite

Jesus told an important story about missing moments when he talked to us about the good Samaritan. Most all of us, whether we are avid readers of the Bible or not, have heard a variation of it in our lifetime. In it, a Jewish man was beaten, robbed, and left to die on the side of the road. Soon a priest and a Levite, two men of importance, walked right by and avoided helping him. Shortly after, a Samaritan came along. Samaritans and Jews disdained one another, but this Samaritan was different from most. As he saw the man bleeding and dying, he stopped everything he was doing to help this stranger who had suffered senselessly at the hands of heartless men.

The extremes to which he showed compassion were unprecedented. He wasn't the first to arrive on the scene, but he was the first responder to offer a lifeline in this man's moment of need. He treated his wounds and transported him out of harm's way to a place he could continue to be cared for. Further seizing the moment, he paid for the man's room and ongoing care long after he was gone. Talk about going the extra mile!

Now, before you judge the priest and the Levite too harshly, let's remember that, just like us, they were real people too. Could it be that other circumstances caused them not to stop and help the man desperately in need? In 1973 social psychologists John Darley and Daniel Batson conducted a study to determine what factors contributed to the reasons some people choose to help others in need and some choose to look the other way.[2] The researchers asked sixty-seven seminary students to give a sermon on the good Samaritan. Unknowingly, the students were actually playing the starring roles in the sermon they were preparing to give.

The study divided the students up into two groups who were subjected to two different sets of conditions. One set of conditions allowed students to deliver their sermons with no rush, while the other hurried them along under stressful circumstances. So, for some of the students, when they arrived to deliver their sermon, they were told that the location had been changed and that they only had minutes to spare to get there on time. The rest of the students were given unhurried conditions, still being asked to go to another location but being assured that they had plenty of time to get there.

As each student walked alone to the other building, he encountered a man slumped in a doorway, eyes closed, moaning, and in obvious distress. The researchers watched from a safe distance to see how each seminary student responded. Would he stop to help the stranger or keep going to deliver his sermon—the one on *the good Samaritan*?

The psychologists found that only 10 percent of the students who were in a hurry bothered to help, while 63 percent of those who felt they had plenty of time actually stopped to assist. Some of the rushing students literally stepped over the distressed man on their way to the next building! The researchers concluded that even students studying to be ministers and preparing to deliver a good Samaritan sermon would continue on course when pressed for time and ignore a person in need. It wasn't callous indifference; many of the conflicted students were simply in a hurry.

> God's grace has the ability to make every moment matter, even the ones we miss.

The priest and the Levite may have kept on walking out of religious indifference, racial disparity, or maybe they were in a hurry too. Whatever the case, we mustn't forget that, as believers, we are held to a higher standard. There is no excuse when it comes to caring for a hurting humanity, no matter what our differences may be or how busy we are. This story should provoke a pause in all of us, causing us to reflect so we, too, can seize these types of moments rather than miss them.

Seizing our moment may be accepting a phone call instead of sending it to voice-mail, or helping an elderly person load his groceries into his car when it's easier to just get in our car and drive away. It may come in the tone of your voice, being intentional about giving someone your undivided attention, or preferring someone else's need above your own. It may be realizing that it's okay for *our plans* to be interrupted by *God's plans*.

So, whether you've had moments that were manipulated, lost, stolen, or simply missed, here is something to remember: there's always hope. God is a redeemer of time. He is a redeemer of moments. Never underestimate that God's grace has the ability to make every moment matter, even the ones we miss.

chapter nine

Rocky Moments

If you've watched any number of movies throughout your lifetime, you know that what separates great from average is the way a director can create a level of suspense such that you, the viewer, feel as if you are a part of the actual scenes. Action movies do this particularly well. Inevitably, the heroes get in a tight spot they have to navigate out of. Perhaps they have to escape from a burning building, cut a wire to a bomb just seconds before it explodes, or jump from a boat to safety before it crashes down a waterfall. The more suspenseful the shots, the more we find ourselves cringing, moving in our seats, and peeking through hands clasped over our faces.

The scenes that get me the most are when the heroes find themselves climbing a steep mountain with no ropes or safety harnesses to protect them. As they take each step, we start to feel the overwhelming sense of anxiety that things may not work out at all. A rock gives way, causing a foot to lose its position. A misplaced grip causes the climber to hang suspended in the air by one hand before dramatically regaining their grasp and continuing the climb. It can go either way: success at the top of the mountain or crashing abruptly on the ground below.

I guess I'm so uneasy watching these moments because subjecting myself to something like a mountain climb is so against my nature. I like knowing I am standing on a firm foundation. I don't like making a step on uneven rocks that could cause me to lose my balance and fall. Still, even though you'll probably never see me climbing a mountain, I've lived long enough to know that rocky places in my personal life are inevitable. And although we know that rocky moments—low moments, if you will—happen to all of us, I've found from years of counseling and pastoring people that not many of us like to talk about them.

There's something about being on a high place, a good place, a firm place that makes us want to tell the world when we are there, yet we retreat into our own silence when we find ourselves wrestling with uncertainties. Truly not missing the moments, though, requires us to embrace, learn from, and go through not only the highest of highs but the lowest of lows. How we handle them makes all the difference.

Moments of Instability

Everyone goes through seasons of hardship, when things more often feel uncertain and overwhelming than peaceful and sure. Wouldn't it be awesome to be able to snap one's fingers, skip these rocky parts of our lives, and go right to the next phase? My answer would be yes, but, unfortunately, that is not the case for any of us. No one is exempt from these moments of turmoil. Times like this can be uncomfortable to say the least, and utterly devastating at their worst, but it is how we respond to the difficulties of these seasons—while we are *in* them—that defines who we become when we emerge *from* them.

Jesus was a great example of how to manage seasons of uncertainty. He knew that his days as friend, mentor, and hero to his disciples would eventually come to an end. The events leading to his death, burial, and resurrection were already in motion, and there was no turning back. I am sure that as the end drew near, so did his feelings of conflict.

> There will always be a war between what you are called to do and what you want to do.

Why would he be conflicted? Because there will always be a war between what you are *called* to do and what you *want* to do. There will always be a war between our flesh and our spirit. Jesus was conflicted because of the impending suffering he knew was coming—suffering on a level no one had ever seen.

Knowing you are facing the most important event in history would be daunting to think about. Knowing the entire event would revolve around *you* dying a cruel death by crucifixion for all mankind? Well, let's just say, that would be enough to have you wringing your hands in prayer while sweating "great drops of blood" (Luke 22:44 NLT). But it would also probably bring some relief to know what you were *about to do* was precisely what you were *born to do*! The purpose, the planning, the reaching and teaching that you had done would finally come to its inevitable conclusion. And yet, the Savior still had to travel through his private Gethsemane to finally arrive at his very public Golgotha.

When reading about his encounter in the Garden of Gethsemane, we are exposed to some of the most human moments we are allowed to see in the life of Jesus. This was not a time when he was healing blinded eyes with all of heaven's authority, raising the dead while ignoring the doubters, or tormenting his haters with his compassionate love of both sinner and saint. This moment was different. This was a moment like none other. This was a moment when Jesus was wrestling with his past, present, and future. He was overwhelmed with unspeakable grief and irrepressible sorrow. His soul was collapsing as he was preparing to absorb the sins of the world. As the pressure of the moment began intensifying, the Bible says he asked God three times if this "cup of suffering" could pass from him.

Have you ever been in a season where you felt

overwhelmed and you asked God to give you a pass on the situation you were about to face? I know I have, and I would dare say some of you who are reading these words right now have done the same. I think it's what we instinctively do when the realities of life are closing in on us, leaving us with feelings of instability.

Recently, my family and I went on a cruise. It was the first time we had ever done this as a family, and we were so excited to share this experience with each other. We even had my husband's parents and siblings sailing with us, so it had the potential to be a fun and relaxing time. This cruise could help us unwind and give us much-needed space to reconnect with each other without the tethers of our personal and professional responsibilities pulling on us.

We strategically chose the month of December so it would be an early Christmas present for the kids and a great ending to our year. We packed, prepared, and proceeded to embark on what we thought would be several days of smooth sailing on the high seas. Boy, were we in for a surprise! This cruise ended up being the rockiest and most unstable journey I have ever been on. I cannot tell you how "un" this vacation was: uncertain, unpredictable, unsettled, and unsteady. No matter if we were docked in the harbor of a beautiful Caribbean island or out in the middle of the ocean, our boat swayed and rocked like a toddler taking her first steps, bobbing and weaving with every wave. And while we were prepared for slight disturbances in the water that typically happen on a cruise, this was by far worse than we were expecting. Needless to say, most everyone in our party was seasick at one time or another. I don't think my husband ever left our cabin!

The swell and dips of the waves and the rough winds caused the cruise ship to roll dramatically. But, during the times when we could make our way to the restaurants or out on the deck, we would watch as the crew just kept on doing their jobs. They provided great service and great entertainment in spite of the troubled waters we were working our way through. While they could sympathize with us over our seasick situation, they had been trained to continue on with a smile even in the midst of the stormy sea.

Not only did they have the training, but they also had experienced these conditions before and knew what to expect to a certain degree. They knew that to panic during these scenarios would only be a detriment to the lives and safety of the passengers and other crew. They made a choice, and it is the same choice we make in rocky moments. We can either recall our training and experiences, anchoring ourselves to what we know is true, or we can let the instability of the moment overtake us.

We need not simply allow ourselves to be at the whims of rough waters, no matter how rough, but we do need to understand the necessity of having an anchor. When a ship is at sea and the captain decides it needs to be docked due to stormy conditions, he cannot just pull into port and hope the ship automatically stays in the right place. Without the proper anchor, it is highly probable the winds and the waves will pull the ship back into the very thing it just pulled out of. The primary role of the anchor is to grip the rock in the sea bed and stabilize the vessel. However, we should be aware of the fact that having an anchor is not a guarantee that the ship will not move. What it does guarantee is that there will be limits to its movement. It may sway, waver, toss, turn, and even pull away from port, but the good news is, it will only go so far!

What I'm telling you today about the ship and its anchor is something I have experienced firsthand. No, I do not *own* a ship with an anchor, but I *am* a ship. I *am* a ship who has known what it's like, more than once, to wonder if and how I will ever get through the rough seas I have found myself in. The good news for me is that I am not moving aimlessly at the mercy of the turbulent winds or stormy situations that beat up against my vessel. I, too, have an anchor that *grips* the rock.

The Rock I am referring to is not just a rock among rocks. No, I am anchored by the Rock, Christ Jesus! He is what gives us hope when everything in our life is shaking. The Bible says, "We have this certain hope like a strong, unbreakable anchor holding our souls to God himself" (Heb. 6:19 TPT). Our "souls" speak of our minds. And when our ship, our hope, or our life grips the Solid Rock, it will anchor our mind. It will stop us from reeling back and forth, in and out, and up and down. It will stop us from staggering at the promises of God. It will stop us from drifting into the depths of depression, despondency, defeat, and despair!

There is nothing like God walking into your room in the middle of the night, in the middle of a storm, while tears are rolling down your face and blinding you from hope. Out of nowhere, he declares, "Peace! Be still." I can't tell you how many times he came to me this way. Yes, *he* came to *me*! When I could not come to him, he came to me. He grabbed my mind, my will, my intellect, and my emotions, and he anchored me just in the nick of time. If you are reading these words today, fighting to withstand the relentless waves that have been beating against your life, please, whatever you do, don't give up. Why throw in the towel when you can throw out the anchor?

Whenever the need arises for the anchor, it always causes a chain reaction. A crew member, usually the captain, recognizes the need for the anchor and orders for it to be lowered. Someone else on the crew must then push the bottom or pull the rope to get the process started. It is never just one person who does it all. This is worth mentioning because when our lives have been disrupted by potentially destructive storms, we often need the help of those who are a part of our crew.

I know for the most part we are pretty tough and some of us are determined to "handle" whatever life throws in our face, but believe me when I say there is something that can break down even the toughest among us. No matter who you are, where you live, what you drive, who you know, or what your financial status may be, life has a way of becoming unstable and overwhelming in the blink of an eye. One phone call, one email, one text message, or one doctor's report has the potential to destabilize and dismantle life as you have known it.

That's how I felt the day my sister Kay, who had been in a battle with cancer for five years, looked me in my eyes and said, "Sheryl, it's time to change how we're praying now, honey." Totally stunned, I stood there, thinking, *What in the world could she mean? Why would she say that? Is her pain becoming unbearable? Is this her way of telling me she knows her life is coming to an end? Is she tired of fighting?* If that was the case, I would have taken the fight to another level on her behalf, because there is absolutely nothing I wouldn't have done for her! She was a pillar in my life! She was a stabilizing force! I was a part of her crew, and she was part of mine. No matter how high the mountaintop God allowed me to stand on, I always wanted to know she was there *with me*. And no matter how deep, dark, or discouraging the valley I might find myself descending into, she always wanted me to know she was there *for me*. She was my ride or die, and she was dying.

To say that I wrestled with her instructions is an understatement. She was insisting that we drop the anchor. I honestly think she was depending on me to help those she loved, along with those who loved her, understand where she was in the fight. She had fought long and hard, but her body was failing. She was growing weaker and thinner by the day. We needed to understand that and face the reality, and we needed to do it while standing with her and grounding ourselves firmly in prayer. We needed to stop trying to outrun the storm and drop the anchor.

We tried to make the best of things. There were times when Kay's strength would return, and she would take a direct flight to Dallas to spend a few days with her Texas family. We would cook for her, love on her, laugh, cry, pray, and gather around the piano and worship with her. We took the time to have fun together, to be sisters, and we shopped till we dropped! I wanted to buy her everything. I was throwing clothes at her left and right.

"Try this one on. It'll be beautiful on you!" She'd say things like, "I don't think that color will work on me," to which I would say, "Are you kidding me?! Of course it will! Just try it on, 'cause I'm the boss of you!" Everything she tried on was perfect! "OMG, Kay, I love it! Do you love it? You gotta love it! You are gorgeous, so we're getting it because I'm the boss of you and I said so!" I joked with her about how, for the first time in our lives, she was smaller than me. She loved that.

I cleaned out my closet every time she came, sending her home with suitcase after suitcase filled with clothes . . . all the while quietly asking God to please let her live long enough to enjoy wearing them. I started calling her my

Barbie, and she would just give me that funny lil' smile of hers. She was as proud to wear the things I gave her as I was for her to have them.

The problem was my "Barbie" was running out of strength long before she could wear all her clothes. Time was changing things. She knew that better than any of us. None of us wanted to hear that and, to a certain degree, many of us were still living in denial. Yet, because of how thoughtful a person she was, she was doing everything she could to prepare us, to anchor us firmly for the moments ahead. The rocky moments. The moments that would shake my faith, my belief systems, my hope, and pretty much everything about my life.

Those little fun moments we had where I would tell her what to do because "I was the boss of her" quickly ended when she spoke the words, "It's time to change the way we pray, honey." Each time those who loved her came by to check on her, I heard them over and over again as she would say, "Tell them how we are praying now, Sheryl." The only thing I could say to that was, "We're praying that God will give her the desires of her heart."

It wasn't easy to pray that prayer. As a matter of fact, it was very painful to pray that prayer, but not long after we began praying it, God answered our prayer. And on Sunday morning, October 8, 2017, God gave my precious sister the desire of her heart when he picked her up and, in a moment, he carried her out of five years of suffering into eternal life! No more pain, no more sickness, no chemo, no radiation, and no more bad doctor's reports. She had been so brave. She had fought a good fight, finished her course, kept the faith, and was on her way to a crown of righteousness that had been laid up with her name on it (2 Tim. 4:7–8).

Losing Kay was a bittersweet moment for me. I was so glad to know she was no longer suffering, but my heart shattered into a million pieces that day because when you love hard you grieve hard. The sweet part came in when I began to understand just how close Jesus is to the broken-hearted. Through it all I'm learning that when a heart breaks it can heal, but it heals differently. I have never been the same. I'm not saying that's a bad thing, but loving and losing Kay changed me.

Those moments hurt, but little by little, I began watching as my hurt turned back into hope. And then . . . seven months and seven days later, in the wee hours of the Tuesday morning after Mother's Day, God slipped into my sweet little mother's room and, just like he'd done with Kay, he picked her up and carried her away to be with him forever. In the blink of an eye, her battle with Alzheimer's was over. I will admit that in those initial hours of losing her I was wondering if God was trying to kill me! Could I take my world being rocked again so soon by another huge loss? *Why me?! Why now?! Why my mom?!* But, then again, why not my mom? As a friend would later summarize in a card to me, "She was a perfect pick for heaven. She is pain-free, care-free, and worry-free. Her memory is fully intact, and she is no longer carrying the burden of an aging body . . . I can only imagine!"

Though I loved hard, and would grieve hard, I was able to not only look at what I had lost in my mom, but to see what I was left with. I was so blessed to have had my mother with me for so many years. She modeled Jesus to me 24–7, and I love that. She left me loaded with things that money can't buy. It would be impossible to list them all, but they are things like the love of a family, a powerful prayer life, stewardship, a work ethic, and her unwavering optimism. All these attributes and more have served as a road map to guide me through the inevitable rocky moments in my life.

Getting Through It

So we've learned we need to drop anchor and put our trust in Jesus when the storms come, but how do we actually do that? How do we get through these moments that can sometimes leave us feeling paralyzed and debilitated? Do we just let low, rocky moments creep into our daily routines and put up with them, hoping they eventually go away, or do we fight back? I'm sure you can already tell that my response to that would be, "We have no choice but to fight back!"

"*How?*" you might ask. It starts with a conscious

decision to survive, to retrain our minds and reshape our reactions when we are confronted by rocky moments.

Before we actually begin healing through it all, we have to remember that one of the primary things destabilizing moments are used for is to steal our faith. Should you ever feel like yours is starting to slip away, you have to fight with all you have to maintain your grip. And even in those moments, when your faith feels like it's on empty, when you have questions, when you don't know what to do next, rest assured that you are *not failing God* in the least simply because your faith is being challenged. In fact, the fluctuations of your faith are as natural as breathing your next breath.

> The fluctuation of our faith doesn't equate to the absence of our faith.

If we're being honest, we spend the majority of our time in the tensions of our highs and lows. Our faith will fluctuate, and that's a reality of life. It's important to know that the fluctuation of our faith doesn't equate to the absence of our faith. In fact, it's quite the opposite.

Try to envision your faith like the stock market. Some days it's up; other days it's down. On the days it is down, just as any Wall Street banker will tell you, don't panic and don't make the mistake of pulling out completely. There's a good chance that the market (and your faith) will be right back up the next day.

There's also a big difference between a temporary low

and a full-blown market crash! Savvy investors will tell you that fluctuations are what actually help the market not get too high and not sink too low. It's a rhythm. And a rhythm, whether in the stock market of your faith or your finances, can be expected. Just remain rock steady, maintain a healthy perspective, and know that Jesus has prayed for you that your faith will fail not (Luke 22:32). Remember, the evidence of trouble doesn't mean the absence of faith. Despite the highs and lows of whatever you may face, God desires us to pass through them with our faith fully intact.

There's No Crying in _____

In the 1992 classic *A League of Their Own*, Tom Hanks plays a rough and somewhat uncaring coach named Jimmy Dugan. He reluctantly decides to coach the first female professional baseball team. One of the most iconic scenes is when Coach Dugan reprimands a player for making a mistake in a game. As a result of his criticism she begins to cry. Dugan responds after seeing her begin to weep, "Are you crying? Are you crying? Are you crying?! There's no crying! There's no crying in baseball!" To this day we still laugh about that scene, and so many people quote it in different contexts, whether referring to crying in sports, or business, or life. And although that might be somewhat true in baseball, it's the furthest thing from true in life.

Never let anyone tell you how to process your pain. Whether you choose to talk through it, journal through it, think, laugh, or cry through it, this is not what really matters. What does matter is that you get through it! You may never get over it, but you must get through it. For some of us this looks like crying. Sometimes crying is essential for getting through some of the most painful moments in life. No matter what Coach Dugan or anyone else has to say about it, cry if you must, and never forget that the Bible says, "They that sow in tears shall reap in joy" (Ps. 126:5 KJV). Often, it's the shedding of our tears that waters the seeds we've sown.

I remember shortly after returning to Dallas after my sister's funeral, we were preparing for our annual Night of Hope Christmas production. For weeks our music and arts department had worked diligently to prepare for our Christmas musical. I can't tell you the anxiety that was running through my body as the program grew closer and closer to the moment I was to take the stage and add my voice to theirs, to culminate what we had declared to be our Year of Hope. "Year of Hope?" Wow! This had been the most hopeless year of my life! The last thing I wanted to do was get up there and hype people up about a *hope* I did not have.

It was my turn to wrap up the program by reminding the people that discouragement, depression, disappointment, and, most of all, hopelessness were defeated by Jesus Christ on Calvary two thousand years ago. However, the gap between what I *needed* to say and what I *wanted* to say felt as big as the Grand Canyon. As a matter of fact, I scared myself a bit that night as I walked toward the pulpit. I really wasn't sure how to bridge that gap. I felt as if my private struggle was about to be put on public display, and it was.

I found myself filtering less and being brutally honest with the audience that night. I told them how disappointed I was with God. How I felt like he could have easily healed Kay, sparing her and all of us who loved her from the gut-wrenching pain that the last few months had taken us through. I had come to the Night of Hope with a thousand questions for which I had no answers. I shared with them a conversation I'd had with God where I told him, "You know I'm not a faker, and I'm not sure that I can continue to tell people you are who I've always told them you are. How can I continue to tell them you are a healer? How can I tell them that you answer prayer? How can I ever again chime in with everyone when they say, 'God is good all the time, and all the time God is good'?!"

My heart was broken, and my faith had been shaken to its very core and was now hanging in the balance. I didn't like where I was. I didn't like how I was feeling. I had never imagined that everything I had ever believed would turn on me. I never imagined that I would ever have to fight and contend for my faith like I was fighting for it now. I wanted to turn back the hands of time. I wanted to go back to simpler days and forget that this season of my life ever existed!

I despised the unstable place I was in. I felt like that ship that had been slapped around by the fiercest winds. These were the rockiest moments I had ever known in my relationship with the Lord. Never had I been overwhelmed with doubt and unbelief to this magnitude. This fight was for real. Would I make it? Would I come out of it? Would I survive this? Would I need to go somewhere and build a new life with a different belief system? How could I explain that to my husband, mother, kids, grandkids, and church? All we had ever known was God! We had depended on him, leaned on him, trusted in him, and stood on his Word for generations. Now it felt like the only thing I could ask him consistently was, "Are you the Christ, or should I look for another?" (Matt 11:3, paraphrased).

There was no doubt that I was in a fight with God for everything I had always taught and been taught, but this was not a fight I wanted to win. That may sound strange to you, but hear me out for a second. No one ever wants to win a fight with God, because winning a fight with God always makes you the loser. Winning this fight, for me, would have ultimately made me lose everything. If all my doubts had turned out not to be doubts at all but actual truths, then everything I had lived, worked, hoped, breathed, and believed for would have been for nothing.

There was so much I didn't understand about where I was and what I was feeling, but the one thing I couldn't deny was the fact that, in spite of it all, I still loved God. I wasn't even sure that I still wanted to love him, but I loved him anyway. I wanted to quit, but my love for him wouldn't let me. I wanted to throw in the towel, but my love for him wouldn't let me. I wanted to run in the opposite direction of everything I had ever known, but my love for him wouldn't let me. I was hopelessly constrained by the love of God.

By his grace, the prayers of the righteous, and a deep-seated desire to want to prove every doubt wrong, I dug my nails in to the rocky place where my hopes had been dashed, and I held on with every ounce of love I had in me. While standing there feeling like the fight could go either way, I opened my mouth and I declared Romans 8:35–39: "I'll let *nothing* separate me from the love of God in Christ Jesus. Neither death, nor life, nor angels, nor principalities, nor powers, nor things present, nor things to come, nor height, nor depth, nor any creature, shall be able to separate me from the love of God in Christ Jesus."

Something happened to me that night. Somewhere between taking the platform and returning to my seat, something anchored me. I found an inner strength that was fueled by a hope I didn't even know I had! The God who is a very present help in the time of trouble had come to help *me*! I thought I was supposed to be helping others, but the reality was he was there to help *me*! He stood up *in* me, *with* me, and *for* me. He gave me the courage to be honest about my reality, and when I took a risk, opened up, and let out the feelings and thoughts that had been running through my mind like it was a treadmill, he instantly reached around all my confusion, apprehending my darkness by the brightness of his light! He did what *only* he could do. Only God could fix this. His voice was the only voice that could talk me off the cliff that my human reasoning had led me to. And, in true Godlike form, he sovereignly began stabilizing everything that was shaking within me.

And I wasn't the only person he helped that night; he also helped many people who were like me. I am still today hearing story after story of people who made the decision that night to denounce the doubts that were trying to discourage them in their lives' destabilizing moments. I don't know you, but I know life and I know God. And if you, like us, should ever find yourself questioning where you are in your journey, or desperately trying to rock steady in the storm, please don't give up! Don't make the mistake of trying to get through this by yourself. Don't stuff your emotions. Emotions are real, and they must be handled. Acknowledge them. Open up, and talk to God about them. I promise, nothing you say will shock him. He already knows how you feel. He is a true friend, and he will help you as you navigate through the rocky moments of life.

The Gift of Compassion

Now, anyone who really knows me knows I am a stabilizer. Whenever I see someone in a crisis, something rises up within me, and I want to do everything in my power to bring balance to the moment and, hopefully, usher in a sense of peace to the situation. Whether through word or deed, I'm in it with you. I do it because I remember what it's like to be in a crisis and in dire need of assurance that everything will turn out okay. And when God brings you through moments such as this, it unlocks a measure of compassion in you that will most likely be with you for the rest of your life.

In some ways, all of us have something in us that triggers our compassion. It kicks in, and we find ourselves donating to a complete stranger's GoFundMe page or babysitting for a single mother who just needs time to run some long-overdue errands. Maybe it's picking up groceries for an elderly neighbor, volunteering at your church, or simply offering emotional support to a friend who has fallen on tough times. Compassion is the very best part of us; however, the key to unlocking that compassion is often found by surviving our own rocky moments.

Have you ever noticed just how many miracles came on the heels of Jesus being "moved with compassion"? He forgave sin and iniquity because of his compassion. He fed the hungry, encouraged those who were sad, loosed those who were bound, comforted the comfortless, and gave hope to the hopeless, all because of compassion. It was his compassion that made him gracious, long-suffering, plenteous in mercy and truth. He healed the sick, cleansed the leper, opened the eyes of the blind, and brought back to life those who were dead! And his compassion was the key to it all.

Whatever you do, whatever you face, whatever life may take you through, never allow it to bankrupt you of your compassion. Never allow it to make you cold and calloused to the point where you lose your ability to feel. Being able to survive the relentless storms in your own life and still be moved with compassion for others is one of the key qualifiers for God to use you in any type of ministry.

Jesus came to earth to live among mankind for thirty-three years so he could be "touched with the feeling of our infirmities" (Heb. 4:15 KJV). He was intentional about it. He went through abandonment, betrayal, mockery, rejection, lies, loss, poverty, pain, and everything else that you and I would ever experience so that, when we came to him for help, he would know what it feels like to be us! And because he knows, he is moved with compassion.

When that type of compassion kicks in, it can make all the difference between a person winning or losing. All the difference between crashing underneath the weight of hardship or carrying it like a champion. And the great thing is, the cycle continues. Just as Jesus' compassion changed everything for us, when we release true compassion to others, it can do for them what an anchor does for a ship: rock them steady in unsteady waters.

When You Least Expect It

Every New Year's Eve at our church, The Potter's House North, we do a big celebration to ring in the new year. We mark it as a time to thank God for all he's blessed us with, say goodbye to the things that may have not gone so well, and look forward to a great new season filled with dreams, aspirations, and possibilities. At exactly midnight, we celebrate with a big countdown filled with confetti cannons firing or balloons dropping. This past New Year's Eve, I requested a balloon drop, because, well, the cannons scared the living daylights out of me a couple of years before. I mean, I knew they were coming—my staff and I had discussed it at length, there were signs on the TV monitors saying they would be firing—and still, when I said, "Happy New Year!" and the loud bang occurred, I felt like I jumped back ten feet off the stage! It's one of those funny ministry moments I'm glad we captured. If you're looking for a little entertainment, you can still see it on my Instagram.[3]

So, in light of the cannon scare in the past, I was definitely #TeamBalloon this year. Our team was in place and knew exactly what to do. At midnight on the dot, they were to pull the strings to release balloons to drop all over the sanctuary, signifying that the new year was here. But something happened around 11:45 p.m. As I was standing on the stage, thanking God for bringing me through absolutely the toughest year of my life, I heard the words, *When you least expect it*. I felt my heart swell with excitement like it does when I know something is being birthed in my spirit. I felt hope and expectation in a place where sorrow and despair had tried to take residence for so long. I wanted our church to feel this too. I wanted them to position themselves to expect God to move, in this new year, even when it was *least* expected!

I remember turning to our production manager on the stage, who had a direct link to our staff controlling the balloons through her headset. "Pull them now," I said. "Now?" she asked, unsure if I really meant to drop them fifteen minutes ahead of time. "Yes, now . . . pull them now." Balloons started to fall everywhere. I could see some of my staff in the crowd scrambling with each other, trying to find out what had happened. People started celebrating well before the clock struck midnight. As I could see the shock on everyone's faces, I grabbed the microphone and declared, "This is going to be a year when God moves when you *least expect it*! Start looking for the unexpected movement of God!"

It became a defining moment in our local church. For weeks and weeks afterward and still to this day, people started telling testimonies of how God intervened on their behalf when they least expected it. I put a huge empty water jug in our conference room and challenged our staff to put a dollar, a quarter, something in it every time God did something unexpected in their life. That jug continues filling up. I can't wait for our Night of Hope in December when we will use the proceeds to bless those who are in need.

So why am I telling you this? I want you to know, at the end of it all, after you do all the right things, after you position your heart in a way to learn and grow from rocky moments, that you still serve a God who is supernatural. Through this book you've learned some very practical things to help you not miss moments. Let me challenge you to also recognize and look for the supernatural at work in you. The hand of the Lord can do more in one touch than a lifetime of our best practices and intentions. Be on high alert, look for unexpected moments, and watch God bring you out of every rocky moment when you *least expect it*!

Conclusion

What I Hope You Never Miss

As we come to the conclusion of our journey through these "moments" together, my sincere prayer is that you've discovered a little more about yourself and an even greater awareness that God, who orchestrates our moments, wants the very best for us. He is so strategic that even in moments that have the potential of knocking us completely off track, he swoops in and works them all together for our good and for his glory.

Moments are recognizable when you train your eye to perceive them. They have distinct traits you have to train your eye for. I overheard two ladies talking while I was waiting for my coffee and couldn't help but laugh at the honesty and realness of their conversation. It went something like this: "Well, I tell my kids all the time, if Mommy is not looking you in the eye when you talk, there's a good chance I'm not listening to a thing you say. And even when Mommy is looking you in the eye, there's still a good chance I'm not listening." I'll admit I chuckled just a bit, because I've had that happen to me. I've been in a conversation and then in midstream wandered off in my mind to somewhere else completely, only to join back in moments later, missing it all! In order to not miss the God moments of our lives, we have to know they exist. Start conditioning yourself to look for these moments to happen at times, and in places, you'd least expect them.

How we prepare for moments will determine how ready we are to fully seize them when they come our way. As Abraham Lincoln put it, "I will prepare and someday my chance will come." As you've noticed throughout this book, I've tried to plead the case that every single day moments are presenting themselves. Part of not missing them is recognizing them, and part is how we are preparing for them before they arrive. I've heard it said, "Downtime is prep time for prime time." I can't tell you how true that is.

What are you doing right now to prepare for a moment that is coming your way? How are you train-ing yourself to better recognize the voice of God? What books are you reading (besides this one, obviously)? What podcasts are you listening to? And, perhaps most importantly, how are you working on your character and your integrity—how are you becoming a better person? You see, if you aren't looking in the mirror on a daily basis and asking God, "Show me how I can improve the real me," I'm afraid you may miss the point of seizing a moment altogether.

Sadly, I see so many people reach and step and claw their way over others in hot pursuit of their next moment. And you know what? Sometimes they get there. But getting there and staying there are two totally different things. What good is it to get to where you've always wanted to be but to turn around and see a trail of broken relationships and broken people you've shattered on your way to your moment? Preparation has so much more to do with how you progress. Become a better person first, and watch God send wave after wave of moments.

I hope you will never miss that there will be times—actually, many times—when you will find yourself waiting and waiting and waiting on moments. Can you discipline yourself enough to be patient in those holding patterns where God simply says, "Not now"? Your ability to wait—and to wait properly—is an indicator to God that you can pass any test laid before you. And let's face it: tests are rarely fun. Just ask any middle or high school student. It was the same for my generation and will be the same for generations to come.

Tests, to those who are taking them, aren't the most pleasant experiences. There are a million other things we'd love to do. Yet they are so important to our growth as believers. Tests can be tricky because they require us to dig deep within ourselves to determine how much we have retained of what we have been taught. They can feel isolating.

Typically, most teachers don't talk much during the test. They are exercising a degree of faith that what they have invested in their students through their teaching has stuck in the corners of their minds and, at the right time, they'll be able to recall and execute what they have learned. Tests are never meant for God to find out where we stand; he knows that already. They are for *us* to know where we stand and where we need to adjust.

If you find yourself going through a testing time, don't just go through it; grow through it! What did you learn in it? What areas did you find yourself strong in? Where were you weak? All those questions help us discover where we need to build more of our faith muscles. If you found yourself fighting at night, losing sleep, and worrying about the unknown during your last test, let it serve as a reminder to you that, when it happens again, you need to be on guard. Protect your mind, and do not let worry get a foothold again. Perhaps you'll do like I do from time to time and tell the Devil, "I'm going to bed! You are not stealing my sleep or my peace of mind!" Don't run from tests; embrace them. See them for what they are, and allow God to make you even stronger through them.

I hope you will never miss that you have been called as a manager of moments. That God entrusts these beautiful experiences to you, and that not missing them is sometimes just the beginning. How you care for, nurture, grow, and at times make new moments happen for others matters so much. How do you take care of the things God has given you? Are opportunities that were once miracles to you now disregarded because you've gone on to bigger and better things? The management of the little, the small, the seemingly insignificant matters to God. It sets us up for God to surprise us with moments we could have never seen coming. Stay faithful, stay diligent, and treat each moment and season with care. How you manage today will be the qualifying factor for what you have the opportunity to manage tomorrow!

When we manage our current moments well, we honor God. Honoring God in the little, everyday things matters. Honoring him in our lives—in our homes, in our jobs—matters. Even if we are not where we want to be in all these areas, we still honor God because honor matters. Honoring the people he places in your life matters, too. Not only those you think can get you where you're going tomorrow, but those who've helped you get where you are today. Those who were patient with you in your immature moments. Those who loved you in your unloveable moments. Those who were good to you in your ungrateful moments. Those who saw the best in you while enduring the worst of you. This may be a great moment to reach out, text, email or call and honor someone who has made a difference in your life. I promise that as you do, God will send that very same honor back from the people you have helped along the way. Honor reciprocates itself!

> How you manage today will be the qualifying factor for what you have the opportunity to manage tomorrow!

And, yes, even as you're on this path of seeing and honoring the moments of your life, inevitably there will be some that you miss. No matter how hard you try to prepare, look for, and react to them well, you will get it wrong from time to time. Missing a moment can cause you to feel such regret, because it can feel like you will never get another shot, opportunity, or chance to seize what you have missed. And the truth of the matter is that, yes, this may be the case. You may never get a chance to land "that job" you wanted or live in "that house," but please hear me clearly today: it does not mean that a better job or a better house isn't in the works. God has a way of balancing the scales and rerouting our courses in such a way that we're ready when opportunities reemerge. And when they do, rest in the fact that the hard work you put in during the in-between moments will make all the difference.

Lastly, I want to remind you that rocky moments are inevitable. Your faith in God, your attendance in church, your prayer life, your ability to worship God in all things *still* will never stop the fact that unstable moments will come your way. But my prayer is that through this book, you have a better understanding that tough times don't last, but tough people do! Remain steady when they come, do *not* lose your faith, and learn and grow from those moments. Lock arms with the root system God has put in your life. Cry when you have to cry; give yourself time to grieve. It does not and will not have the power to overtake you. You serve a God who has himself experienced every low moment you will go through. The Bible is full of examples where Jesus experienced emotions of exhaustion, anger, sorrow, and frustration. "For we have not an high priest which cannot be touched with the feeling of our infirmities; but was in all points tempted like as we are" (Heb. 4:15 KJV). And in his understanding of our struggles, he is our faithful anchor.

Not missing our moments will require different levels of faith from us, some levels more difficult than others. View your faith as a muscle you need to exercise every day, and don't be afraid to ask yourself what areas of faith need to be worked on. Remember, faith isn't a denier of situations, but it chooses to see things for what they could and should be. Personally, having faith in the moments means that I can look at not enough and call it more than enough because by faith I believe things will get better.

By faith I believe my perspective will get better. My decision-making processes will get better. My career will get better. My ability to manage finances will get better. My relationships, my marriage, and my family will get better. Why? Because I believe. I will seize every moment to go after what I am believing for by faith. Sometimes it takes every ounce of faith you have to just ask. But, I want to challenge you from this moment forward to ask God for what you need by faith.

When I think about having the

> Faith isn't a denier of situations, but it chooses to see things for what they could and should be.

faith to ask, I'm reminded of what happened late one night with my grandkids. It's not unusual for me to receive a FaceTime call from my daughter Nina late at night. I always love saying goodnight to my grandchildren, and especially to my littlest ones, Mason and Mariah. On one particular night around ten o'clock when I answered, Nina simply said, "Tell her," then handed the phone to Mariah.

As Mariah came onto the screen, I asked, "What do you want to tell me, baby?"

She was crying to the point that I could barely understand her, so I finally told her to give the phone to her mommy.

Nina got back on the phone with me, and I asked her, "What's she crying about?"

Nina said, "She's crying for a *cupcake*!"

She began to describe how Mariah had been asking for a cupcake for several minutes and, as a result of not getting one, well, she'd had a good ole-fashioned meltdown.

My maternal wisdom kicked in, and, as any grandmother worth her salt would do, I said, "Why don't you just give her a cupcake?" Seemed simple enough.

"Because I don't have any," Nina explained.

I went through my entire snack list: "Well, then get her a cookie, or a popsicle, or grapes or something." My level of wisdom was at an all-time high here.

"I don't have any of those things," she explained further. "Plus, it's ten o'clock at night. She doesn't need anything sweet before bed."

I knew what I had to do next. "I'll be there in a minute with some cupcakes."

"*No, Mom . . .* no cupcakes."

"Then why did you call me? I can't just watch her cry and not help her if it's within my power to!"

Nina's response once again was, "*No, Mom!* She's going to be just fine."

But my mind was already made up. Because Mariah had asked, I hung up the phone and off I went to the nearest grocery store. I found myself putting everything closely resembling a cupcake in my cart. Cupcakes, cookies, popsicles, gummy bears, doughnuts, and cereal (sweetened cereal, I might add), and all of it was quickly on its way to Mariah's house, hand-delivered by "GeGe" herself! *No Uber necessary!*

I hurried over and rang the doorbell. Nina opened it and greeted me with "*Mom . . .* you did not just do this!"

Oh yes, I did! I carried all my purchases into the house and laid them out on the kitchen counter. Nina was appalled!

I said, "Where is she?"

To which she replied, "She's already in bed. Thanks for bringing all of this, Mom, but you really didn't have to. Just leave it here, and I'll give her some of it tomorrow."

I smiled and said, "You're welcome, but I did have to because I'm a GeGe and it's my job!"

We both laughed. I had to stick my head into the room as I was preparing to leave just to see my little

M&Ms. Much to my surprise, both Mariah and Mason were wide awake. Of course I had to say something to them and, wouldn't you know it, I just happened to have two little cupcakes with white icing hidden in my hand. When Mariah saw what I was holding, she lit up like the Christmas tree on Rockefeller Plaza, sat straight up, and smiled from ear to ear . . . and so did Mason! We sat there on the bed as I fed them by hand, one bite at a time. I wanted to make sure they got every single piece, while ensuring no crumbs would be left behind as evidence. Then I tucked them back in and walked away the hero.

For those of you who might be asking why I would do such a thing, well, my first answer is, "'Cause I could!" Now, granted, I wouldn't do that every time (for a thousand reasons I don't need to mention here, because I'm sure you all already know), but on that particular night I felt like it was a moment I didn't want to miss. I needed to be a *hero*, Mariah needed a *hero*, and, boom, there you have it . . . the *sweetest* match made in heaven (pun intended)!

The second reason I did it was simply because she asked me to. And because she *asked*, I *answered*. Now, there were a lot of obstacles between her ask and my answer, but none of them were as big as my love for her. And because of that, I seized the moment and Mariah had her (cup) cake and ate it too! Love made me jump over every hurdle to capture a moment when I could hand-deliver the desire of her heart, and neither one of us will ever forget it.

Never ever, ever underestimate the power of a simple

ask. The Bible says, "You do not have because you do not ask" (James 4:2). It's not your job to figure it all out. It's not your job to make it happen, but it *is* your job to *ask.* You're the child; he's the Father. It's your moment. Don't miss it. Just ask.

Acknowledgments

To my wonderful husband, Joby, you have made the last forty-three years of my life the best years of my life. Your affirming touch has made me brave. You have helped me to recognize that my words are valuable, and without any hesitation you've always made space for my voice to be heard. Thank you for all the dreams you've made come true and the many that still lie ahead for us. I treasure the moments with you.

To my family: Lana, Marc, McKenzie, Ryan, Tina, Chris, Jaden, Josiah, Judah, Nina, Travis, Sydney, Isaiah, Mariah, and Mason. Thank you for the many times I have walked through the doors of home and the gift of your presence absorbed my exhaustion, weariness, and even my grief. You have spent your love on me and because of that, I am rich.

To Pastor Donald and Mary Lou Brady, thank you for loving us and covering us with the mantle of prayer. We are who we are by the grace of God and your prayers. I love you both from the bottom of my heart! I couldn't have asked for a better father- and mother-in-law/love!

Bishop T. D. Jakes: Over the years, I've learned that people can handle the uncertainty of tomorrow when they trust the leader that is within their life today. You've been that for me for thirty years. Thank you for being my leader, thank you for not leaving me to be mediocre and thank you for all that you've sacrificed so I could gain all that God has allowed me to gain. You are an icon of integrity, leadership, friendship, fatherhood, and so much more. Your willing spirit to share what you have learned throughout your journey of life is nothing short of amazing to me, not to mention rare. You have talked me from weakness into strength, from barrenness to fruitfulness, from nothing into something. The knowledge you have given me has been one of the greatest assets in my life.

First Lady Serita Jakes: If I could build a palette of words that describe you, they would be words like *loyal, graceful, wise, stable, protective, pure,* and *patient*—to name a few. Thank you for making room in your heart for my family. From day one your tender embrace has mirrored the undefeatable force of love. You are the true definition of a safe place and I will always love you.

To my Potter's House North church family: Your unending hunger and thirst after the heart of God continually pushes me to be a better follower of Christ and ultimately a better leader. Your faithfulness to God's house while allowing me to care for the family in my own house is something I will always cherish. Thank you for your healing hugs and sharing your stories of grief with me. You have taught me in seasons of loss that we not only need God's promises, but we need God's people. You have sustained me and given me room to heal and the space to become whole again.

Rose Horne, anyone who says, "A rose is a rose is a rose" has not met my Rose. When God gave me you, he gave me the most beautiful Rose in his garden. You model the commitment to consistency like none other. Thank you for the countless laughs, pats on the back, brainstorming sessions, miles traveled, and the late-night runs to the throne of grace on my behalf. People will never know just how many times you have quietly coached me across the finish line. You are a gift to me that I will be forever thankful for.

Marc Jeffrey, thank you for your tireless efforts to make this vision a reality. Thank you for being the eyes that saw the finished work that people are holding in their hands today. I really appreciate the times you sat in the coffee shops trying to help me articulate the posture of my heart. I appreciate the way you were able to see it through even when life's obstacles seemed insurmountable. You have a creativity and innate ability to make impossible situations seem possible. Thank you for sharing your gifts of creativity, tenacity, and sheer determination on my behalf. They are something I will value always and God will honor eternally.

Apostle Bryan Meadows, thank you for lending me the gift of your magnificent mind. Your contribution to this book was invaluable.

Thank you, Anna Bodmer (my real-life angel), Cinthia Ortiz (my mom's real-life angel). To my friends Roberta Pridemore, Dottie Compton, and Sharon Fox, who shared with me timely words of wisdom that brought me through real, raw moments.

Jan Miller and Shannon Marven: What a warm touch you both bring to the often cold world of business. I feel so blessed to be a part of the Dupree Miller and Associates family.

Nelson Books: In the world of business often the bottom line is the only line that counts. Your care for me as a person allowed me time and space to heal from some of the greatest losses I have ever experienced. You let me know that who I was mattered more than what I did. In spite of detours and delays, thank you for helping me not to miss this moment.

Thank you to my extended family and friends, those of you who have lit up my life in dark seasons with your words of encouragement. Only God knows how much I cherish each and every one of you.

Notes

1. "How Success is Like a Chinese Bamboo Tree," Matt Morris (blog), accessed September 11, 2019, https://www.mattmorris.com/how-success-is-like-a-chinese-bamboo-tree/.
2. J. M. Darley and C. D. Batson, "From Jerusalem to Jericho: A Study of Situational and Dispositional Variables in Helping Behavior," *Journal of Personality and Social Psychology* 27 (1973): 100–108, http://faculty.babson.edu/krollag/org_site/soc_psych/darley_samarit.html.
3. Sheryl Brady (@sherylbrady), Instagram, January 1, 2016, https://www.instagram.com/p/BAAaI1UO-VW/?igshid=240m0ox84uwb.

About the Author

Sheryl Brady serves as the pastor of The Potter's House of North Dallas. She has been a featured speaker at some of the nation's largest conferences, including MegaFest, Woman Thou Art Loosed, and the iconic Women of Faith tours. She also holds the distinct honor of being the first and only female speaker at ManPower, the men's conference hosted by Bishop T. D. Jakes. Pastor Brady is a staple on faith-based television networks, and she has been featured as a columnist for the *Washington Post*, *Fox News*, and other nationally recognized publications. Pastor Brady and her husband, Bishop Joby Brady, make their home in Dallas, Texas.